Golf is a good walk spoiled. MARK TWAIN *Palmer came along at the right time for golf, but Palmer also came along at the right time for Palmer. These things are always a confluence of person and time. Red Barber was indisputably great. But if a young Red Barber came along today, he wouldn't have the same impact because radio isn't as important as it used to be, and there'll never be another team like the Dodgers in a place called Brooklyn in a time like the post-World-War-Two era. Muhammad Ali is probably the single greatest figure in sports history. Certainly, if Ali came along today, he'd still be a great fighter, he'd still be charismatic; but as a phenomenon, maybe he'd be more like Michael Jordan. Now a lot has been said about Palmer being the perfect person to carry golf on television. And it's true, if Arnold Palmer hadn't come along, golf might not have leapt into the television era. But eventually it would have gotten there because the medium is too strong for any sport to ignore. So without taking anything away from Arnold, I think television probably did more for him than the other way around. And television in those days did a lot for a lot of athletes. It's more of a force now than it was then, but there was something special about the blending of sports and television in the early 1960s. The guys who came along during that transition period between sports on the radio and the full-blown television era had the best of both worlds. There was an innocence from the previous era, enough TV for the public to get familiar with them, yet not so much exposure that their mystique was ruined. It was the perfect combination for apocryphal stories and creating legends.* BOB COSTAS *When I was visiting Palmer in Orlando, there was a new member at the club. And the word was out that maybe he was crooked. Some of the members thought so, anyway. And Palmer made a point of playing with him that day to see what he was like. He wanted to size him up over 18 holes because, as far as Arnold is concerned, golf is a test of*

character. There are always excuses on a golf course if you want them. You can always cheat if that's what you have in mind. And to Arnold's way of thinking, if you cheat at golf, then you cheat in business. If you're a jerk on the course, then you're a jerk in the rest of life. So Arnold played with him, and he thought he was fine. RICK REILLY *All America had this image of Palmer taking a cigarette out of his mouth, throwing it on the green to putt, and then sticking it back in his mouth again. It was golf's equivalent of Bogart and Bacall. And it seems odd now to think of a cigarette as an athletic totem, but back then it was sexy. Palmer with a cigarette was like those old convertible ads with a beautiful woman sitting in the front seat and her scarf blowing in the wind.* FRANK DEFORD *Sam Snead will fly anywhere in my plane with me. Sam's not as worried about the danger as he is about saving money.* ARNOLD PALMER *If someone wants to compare the distractions and the pressure on golfers with what goes on for other athletes, that's fine by me. A baseball player strikes out four times in a game, and he still gets paid. A golfer gets nothing if he plays poorly. We get nothing if we're out with an injury. Nobody puts us on a train or plane and gives us a ticket to get to the next stop. Do you understand what I'm saying? Can you imagine what would happen if Barry Switzer told the Dallas Cowboys, "Okay, guys. I want you to be in San Francisco next Friday. Get there on your own." How many of them do you think would make it?* LEE TREVINO *When I met Arnold, he was different from what I'd expected him to be. There was no Mr. Bigshot; he couldn't have been nicer. At the time, I assumed he was being friendly because he was recruiting me to come work with him as his pilot, but after a while I learned that's just the way he is. In the air, when Arnold was in the left seat, he was in charge of the plane and he told me what to do. And when I was in the left seat, it was the other way around. He was a*

good pilot, but there was one incident I remember. We'd been in Chicago and had a disagreement about something that wasn't important, but at the time it aggravated both of us. We had a few words on the plane coming back. Arnold was in the left seat, and I could see he wasn't doing as good a job as he'd normally do. We got to Latrobe around midnight. It was pouring rain; the clouds were very low. Arnold had to try several times before his approach was properly lined up. And then he came in and landed the plane short. It hit in the mud and sort of bounced up onto the runway. I told him, "I think you landed short." He said, "No, I didn't." And the next morning, when we got up early to fly to New York, we still weren't talking to each other. I was in the left seat. So when we taxied down the runway to take off, I pointed the headlights toward some ruts in the mud just beyond the runway, and said, "It looks like someone landed short last night." Arnold thought about that for a moment. And then he said, "I really screwed that up, didn't I?" DARRELL BROWN *One thing I've learned over time is, if you hit a golf ball into water, it won't float.* ARNOLD PALMER *I remember one particular incident at the Jackie Gleason Inverrary Classic. I was covering the 15th hole for CBS, which was a par-5 dogleg to the left. On Palmer's second shot, as was typical of him, he was trying to reach the green, but his ball went to the right and hit a woman in the head. It was a long shot, so it took him a while to reach the green. When he got there, the medical staff was tending to the woman. She was lying on a blanket, and an ambulance was en route. I was looking down from the tower, and it seemed to me that she was seriously hurt. Then Arnold came striding up, went over to the blanket where the woman was lying, knelt down, and kissed her on the forehead. And that woman came up off the blanket like she'd been healed. It was as though the Messiah had healed her. And she stayed to watch the rest of the tournament.* PAT SUMMERALL

I will not play when lightning is threatening. The rules say that any time you feel threatened you can stop. And I've always had a great feeling for wanting to get as far away as possible from lightning. ARNOLD PALMER *My dad argued with his father a lot, so I think there are times he likes it that he has a daughter who argues with him. Only he wishes that at the end of each argument I'd say, "Daddy, you're completely right." But I'm an adult. I'm entitled to my own beliefs, and I don't agree with the way he thinks about a lot of things. And sometimes what angers me is not that we disagree, but that he doesn't seem to care how I feel; that I have to listen to how he feels and weather his anger and his passion as though they were Gospel, and he never really listens to me. On the telephone, even today, if he gets mad, I have the feeling he's about to reach through the phone wires and grab me by the throat, because there's that physical aura about him. Still, I have to tell you, whenever someone comes up to me and says, "Oh, your father is Arnold Palmer; I've seen him on television; I really admire him," I've always felt I could honestly say that, if they ever met him, they'd find him larger than life and be twice as enamored of him. He's everything that people who admire him think he is. I've met a lot of famous people where I asked myself, "Is that all there is to him?" But people who meet my dad are never disappointed. He's not a sham. He is what he seems to be. To me the important things about my father are the good things. His energy, his enthusiasm, his sense of loyalty, his love of family. I don't see the world from the same perspective that he does, but even now, there are very few important situations that arise where I don't ask myself how he would handle the situation. And I'd rather have him be the way he is and keep his good qualities than have him change and lose what I love about him. And I do love him; he's very special. I think he's terrific in a lot of ways.* PEG PALMER WEARS *That looks like good exercise, but what's the little white ball for?* ULYSSES S. GRANT

ARNOLD PALMER

A PERSONAL JOURNEY

by

THOMAS HAUSER

with the cooperation of Arnold Palmer

CollinsPublishersSanFrancisco

A Division of HarperCollins*Publishers*

AN OPUS BOOK

For
HONEY SHIELDS AND ANNE FERGENSON TEALL,
TWO OF MY FAVORITE PEOPLE

BOOKS BY THOMAS HAUSER

Non-Fiction
Missing
The Trial of Patrolman Thomas Shea
For Our Children (with Frank Macchiarola)
The Family Legal Companion
The Black Lights: Inside the World of Professional Boxing
Final Warning: The Legacy of Chernobyl
Muhammad Ali: His Life and Times
Muhammad Ali: Memories
Arnold Palmer: A Personal Journey
Fiction
Ashworth & Palmer
Agatha's Friends
The Beethoven Conspiracy
Hanneman's War
The Fantasy
Dear Hannah
The Hawthorne Group

First published in 1994 by CollinsPublishersSanFrancisco, 1160 Battery Street, San Francisco, California 94111-1213

Produced and created by Opus Productions Inc., 300 West Hastings Street, Vancouver, British Columbia, Canada V6B 1K6

Library of Congress Cataloging-in-Publication Data:
Hauser, Thomas.
      Arnold Palmer: a personal journey / by Thomas Hauser, with the cooperation of Arnold Palmer.
        p. cm.
   ISBN 0-00-255468-2
     1. Palmer, Arnold, 1929-   .   2. Golfers – United States – Biography.
     I. Palmer, Arnold, 1929-   . II. Title.
GV964.P3H38 1994
796.352' 092--dc20
[B]   CIP 94-16172

Printed and bound in China
10 9 8 7 6 5 4 3 2 1

CONTENTS

Preface

IN JUNE 1992, I was approached by representatives of Arnold Palmer and asked if I'd be interested in writing a book about Palmer's life. The invitation came on the heels of my having authored *Muhammad Ali: His Life And Times*. Following the success of that project, I'd been offered and declined numerous "celebrity" books. But the thought of working with, and learning more about, Palmer appealed to me. Unlike Ali, Palmer isn't thought of as a social, political, or religious figure. But his impact on golf, his role in redefining the economics of sports, and his influence as an American icon have been enormous.

With the possible exception of Babe Ruth, no athlete ever did as much for a sport as Arnold Palmer did for golf. During the course of his professional career, he has won 92 tournaments; 61 of them on the PGA tour. He was the first golfer to reach the million-dollar mark in tour earnings, and the first four-time winner of the coveted Masters championship. In a sense, he was a contradiction; "everyman" in an elitist sport. His style of play was, "Hit it hard; go find it; and hit it hard again." Arnie's Army (as his fans were known) expected him to find trouble on the golf course; and then they expected him to play the role of cavalry soldier riding over the hill to save himself from disaster. Palmer at his best viewed lakes, streams, sand bunkers, and trees as nuisances, not hazards. He was the most exciting personality in the history of golf, and for many Americans, their first golf hero.

Prior to Arnold Palmer's emergence, the American public had relatively little use for golfers. At one end of the spectrum, there were touring pros, who were regarded by many as simple hustlers. And the pros didn't just hustle golf; some of them played pretty good pool too. And 180 degrees removed, there was country-club golf, played almost exclusively by the privileged rich. Americans acknowledged that golfers were skilled, but refused to accept them as genuine athletes. The game had too little action, was too controlled and slow. And then along came Palmer; vibrant, charismatic, daring; with blacksmith's forearms and unique good looks, swinging from the heels like Jack Dempsey and Babe Ruth. Arnold Palmer losing a golf tournament was more interesting than almost anyone else winning. He stirred passions and created a sense of sharing his adventures on a golf course in a way that no other golfer ever had. He obviously enjoyed fans in the gallery, and they in turn felt his emotions and were involved in every stroke. He was the first golfer the American public truly cared about, and that appeal carried across class lines. Men liked the way Palmer looked; they thought he was a man's man. Women found him equally charming; handsome, magnetic and strong. Arnold Palmer made golf seem like an American game, and he was responsible for a whole new audience becoming interested in golf.

But Palmer's impact extended far beyond the golf course. He revolutionized the economics of sports. Arnold Palmer was the first athlete to parlay success on the playing field into lucrative endorsement contracts. With the aid of Mark McCormack, he virtually invented the role of the athlete-entrepreneur and created a massive corporate empire. It's not just golfers who are indebted to Palmer today. Michael Jordan, Joe Montana, Wayne Gretzky, Bo Jackson, every athlete with multimillion-dollar endorsement income can trace the roots of his or her financial success to Palmer. No sports figure has ever been more thoroughly marketed, exhibited, licensed and promoted. And the most extraordinary aspect of Palmer's commercial appeal is its longevity. For 30 consecutive years, he was the top grossing athlete in the world in terms of endorsement income. Finally, in 1991, Michael Jordan surpassed him. But at age 64, Palmer still ranks second. And despite having been responsible for opening the floodgates to commercialism in sports, his essence as a competitor has never been compromised. For despite his warmth and considerable grace, Arnold Palmer is a warrior. No amount of poise or humor has ever been able to mask the intensity and determination with which he goes about his craft. Palmer on the golf course radiates decency, but also an all-consuming desire to win.

In sum, for many, Arnold Palmer epitomizes The American Dream and mirrors what Americans like to think of themselves. He's bold, charismatic, a bit impatient, a winner; a man who identifies with his home town, has been married to the same woman for 39 years, succeeds at everything he has ever done, and still seems like a regular guy. Palmer is every mother's loving son and every man's best friend. He's the boy next door with the all-American smile; confident but not arrogant; reassuring and fun. And for more than three decades, he has been a symbol. In the early 1960s, he seemed to blend with images of John F. Kennedy, excitement and youth.

Then the decade turned violent. America was torn apart by political assassinations, urban riots and Vietnam. But "Arnie" remained "Arnie," and resisted the tide. Athletes like Bill Russell, Jim Brown and Arthur Ashe challenged what they believed was wrong with the prevailing American orthodoxy. But Palmer continued to personify everything that he and middle America thought was right. At a time when Muhammad Ali refused induction into the United States Army, and John Carlos and Tommie Smith marked the 1968 Olympics with upraised fists, Arnold Palmer continued to evoke images of America the way Dwight Eisenhower, Norman Rockwell and John Wayne wanted it to be. And the qualities that led millions of people to think of him as "The Quintessential American" endure to this day. Very few athletes hold onto their humility when they become great and retain their magic when they grow old, yet Palmer has done both.

Arnold Palmer: A Personal Journey is an attempt to place Palmer's accomplishments in context and promote a clearer understanding of the values by which he has lived his life. This isn't a book about my opinions, which differ in many respects from his. Rather, it's an attempt to show him as he was and is today. There's a tendency to endow society's heroes with superhuman attributes, and I've done my best on the following pages to separate myth from reality. Arnold himself would be the first to admit that he has his share of flaws. But he's a good person, and one of his nicest qualities is that he's a man without pretense. I saw that for myself in December 1992 when we were together for the first time. I had journeyed to Orlando to begin the process of interviewing him for this book. Our first session was scheduled for early morning, so I flew in the night before and checked into the lodge at Bay Hill, where Arnold and his wife, Winnie, keep their winter home. After I unpacked, I went downstairs for dinner and was seated by the head waitress. Arnold, Winnie and two other couples were midway through their meal at the next table.

I had never met Arnold and Winnie Palmer. All of the previous negotiations for this book had been conducted between myself and Arnold's representatives at IMG. I thought of introducing myself, but decided not to. In part, that was because the Palmers were enjoying what was obviously a social occasion and I didn't want to intrude. Also, I thought it would be fun to play the proverbial "fly on the wall." The next day, I was introduced to Arnold and Winnie. They showed me around Bay Hill; I began the process of interviewing for this book; and that afternoon I walked with Arnold while he played 18 holes of golf. Then, after drinks at their home, we went to the Bay Hill Lodge for dinner. Arnold and Winnie sat at the same table as the night before, only this time, I was with them. And what I remember best about the evening is, Arnold talked and acted the same as he had the previous night. So many people, celebrities in particular, have a variety of faces that they exchange to suit their need of the moment. But Arnold Palmer has one face. There's nothing phony about him. With Arnold Palmer, what you see is what you get.

THOMAS HAUSER
New York, N. Y.

Part One

WHEN THE WORLD
WAS YOUNG

From a 1953 victory;
the Ohio State Amateur trophy.

GAMES SIMILAR TO GOLF
HAVE BEEN PLAYED THROUGHOUT THE WORLD

over the centuries, but Scotland is generally considered to be the cradle of modern golf. By the mid-1400s, the sport had become so popular in the highlands that it was thought to be interfering with the practice of archery, which was essential to defending the realm. Thus, in 1457, Parliament passed a law requiring that all male citizens gather quarter-annually for archery training and further decreed that at these gatherings, "Golfe be utterly cryit doun and nocht usit."

Initially, the game was played with crude wooden balls. In the 1600s, thin leather balls stuffed with feathers were introduced, but these "featheries" were expensive, lost their shape after several rounds of play, and were useless when wet.

In the mid-1700s, the world's first golf clubs were established in Scotland, and a class of professionals who gave instruction and crafted golf equipment was born. The sport was transported across the Atlantic Ocean during the Revolutionary War, but was played only sporadically in its new surroundings until 1888 when the St. Andrew's Golf Club of Yonkers was formed. Thereafter, the game took hold in North America, and by 1929, the year Arnold Palmer was born, there were more than 5,000 golf courses in the United States.

There are many ways to analyze golf, but whichever is chosen, it's clear that the dimensions of the sport are awesome. A golfer typically has four swings to hit a tiny ball 420 yards into a hole

Facing page: A young Arnold Palmer hones the
swing that would become his trademark.

he can't see when he starts. Along the way, he must deal with trees, brooks, sand traps, hills, and whatever else lies in his path. On an average course, he's expected to move the ball from tee to green on 18 separate occasions, using no more than a total of 36 strokes. Another 36 strokes are allotted for putting the ball into the hole once it has landed on the green.

There's a thin line between being a good golfer and a great one, but the best golfers share a variety of traits – strength, hand-eye coordination, concentration, and judgment. When a professional golfer drives off the tee, it's done with more power than the average person can imagine. The head of the club as it comes to the ball is traveling at close to 110 miles per hour. Club and ball are in contact for roughly four 10-thousandths of a second, after which the ball is launched into space at 180 miles per hour. Walking down the fairway preparing for his next shot, a golfer isn't focusing on the beautiful surroundings or crowd nearby. Rather, he's considering the direction in which the grass has been cut, the altitude he's playing at, and a dozen other factors that will determine which club he uses and where he will try to place his next shot.

There's always pressure. Every sport has moments where a game can be won or lost. But in golf, each shot has the potential to eliminate a

Palmer was born in Latrobe, Pennsylvania and lived in a house that bordered the Latrobe Country Club. It was there that his father taught him the game.

competitor from serious contention in a tournament. Every round, every hole, every swing is crucial. A golfer who covers hundreds of yards by perfectly executing rocket-like shots can lose everything by missing a three-foot putt. In some ways, the demands of the sport are similar to those involved in balancing on a high wire. Fierce competitiveness must be filtered through a technique akin to releasing emotion through an eye-dropper. The game is as much mental as physical. The ball is inert. It simply sits there, waiting to be hit. Golf isn't like baseball, where the batter doesn't know whether a fastball or curve is coming. It's not like tennis, where a competitor hits the ball and finds it whizzing back at 120 miles per hour. There are no referees to blame; no opponents to thwart a good shot. There's the golfer, his ball, and the laws of physics. The challenge is pure – the golfer against the course and his own standard.

Arnold Palmer loves the challenge of golf. It has been central to his life for almost 60 years. Palmer's roots are in Latrobe, Pennsylvania, a small steel town in the foothills of the Allegheny Mountains, 30 miles southeast of Pittsburgh. In 1921, the Latrobe Electric Steel Company built a nine-hole golf course. When the job was done, one of the construction workers, Milfred J. "Deacon" Palmer, was kept on as a member of the grounds crew. He taught himself how to play golf, and several years later was promoted to greenskeeper. Then, during the Great Depression, when the club could no longer afford both a greenskeeper and a club pro, he was given both jobs.

Arnold Palmer was born on September 10, 1929, the first child of Deacon and Doris Palmer. "Some of my earliest memories," he recalls, "are of riding around the club on a tractor with my father. When I was three, he made a special set of golf clubs for me, and then he taught me how to hold them. I was lucky; I learned to hold a club the right way when I was young, so the proper grip has always been second nature to me."

The Palmers lived in a small frame house near the fifth hole of the Latrobe Country Club. Doris Palmer kept the pro-shop books and oversaw the family finances. When Arnold was two, his sister Lois Jean was born. "Living on the edge of a golf course wasn't in style back then," Lois Jean remembers. "The families that had money lived in town. The only rooms in our house with heat were the kitchen and living room (which had a fireplace). We always had enough to eat, but I can still hear Daddy saying,

Five-year-old Arnold wielding a sawed-off ladies' driver.

'By God; if you put that on your plate, you'd better eat it.' Daddy was a tough taskmaster. He'd had polio when he was a boy. One of his legs was shorter than the other, and I think that made him more demanding. Whatever we achieved, he always thought we could do better. Arnie was a fantastic older brother; very protective, always looking after me. The only complaint I had about him was, I always fixed him up with my friends on dates, but he'd never let any of his friends date me. He was a good speller in school and very good in math. But he didn't like the other subjects and didn't really work at them."

Golf professionals in the 1930s weren't particularly respected by the club members they served. Rather, they were often looked upon as servants, and Deacon Palmer endured his share of frustration. He was a physical man who sometimes drank too much, and he was hard on Arnold in ways that aren't part of the Palmer legend. He and his wife considered having more children, but it was a dozen years before they felt secure enough financially to have a third child. In 1944, their second son, Jerry, was born. Four years after that, Doris Palmer gave birth to Sandy, their second daughter.

Meanwhile, although Arnold was an indifferent student, he excelled at golf. At age seven, he broke 100 for 18 holes. He was caddying at 11 and repairing clubs at 14. At times, the barrier between club members and non-members weighed heavily on him. He wasn't allowed to play on the Latrobe Country Club course, except early in the morning before members arrived or late in the evening after they'd retired for the night. The swimming pool was always off limits, as were the dining room, locker room, and club lounge. "It was frustrating," he later recalled. "I was raised in a country club atmosphere, but I was never able to touch it. It was like looking at a piece of cake and knowing how good it was, but not being able to take a bite."

Palmer kept on top of his game during his three-year service with the U.S. Coast Guard.

Palmer won the Pennsylvania State High School Championship twice; then enrolled at Wake Forest College on a golf scholarship. "He was still a mama's boy," Lois Jean remembers. "Not a sissy; I don't mean that. But he always tried to look after his mother, and he wasn't used to being away from home. When Sandy was born, mother was almost 40, which was old in those days to be having a child. And Arnie hitchhiked home from Wake Forest just to make sure everything was all right."

Arnold's years at Wake Forest were among the happiest of his life. He was a two-time winner of the Southern Conference Championship and two-time National Intercollegiate Medalist. There were lots of girls and a lot of parties. Then, in 1950, his best friend, Buddy Worsham, was killed in a car accident. The loss shook Palmer to his core and, coupled with declining grades, led him to drop out of college. He enlisted in the Coast Guard, received an honorable discharge after three years' service, and was readmitted to Wake Forest but left again without graduating after one semester. Uncertain as to what to do with his life, he returned to Cleveland, where he'd been stationed in the Coast Guard, and took a job as a paint salesman. Golf was still very much on his mind, but he was unwilling to follow the path taken by his father. "Back then, the golf pro wasn't even admitted to his own clubhouse," he would say later. "And I was too proud to live my life as some kind of second-class citizen."

Then came a defining moment – Palmer's triumph in the 1954 United States Golf Association Amateur Championship. The tournament was held at The Country Club of Detroit on a course designed by the legendary Robert Trent Jones. Palmer played eight matches, including a semifinal

Palmer's career would be made in part on his ability to successfully scramble from difficult places, as seen here during the 1954 USGA Amateur Championship.

battle against Edward Meister, a veteran of 13 USGA Amateur Championship tournaments, that went three holes past the normal 36-hole limit. In retrospect, it was the Palmer-Meister pairing that provided the most prophetic moment of the tournament. Meister had parred the 36th hole, and Palmer was facing a five-foot side-hill putt. If he made it, the match would continue. If he missed it, he'd be eliminated from play. Palmer studied the putt for what seemed an eternity; then stroked it firmly into the hole. "I waited until I was sure I would make it," he said afterward.

The final match was played on August 28, 1954. Palmer's opponent was Robert Sweeny, a 43-year-old investment banker and socialite from Sands Point, New York, who owned vacation homes in Palm Beach and the Riviera. Herbert Warren Wind, now the dean of American golf writers, remembers, "The contrast in their backgrounds was obvious; and quite frankly, just about everyone wanted Arnold to win. He hadn't come to looking you in the eye quite as forcefully and gripping your hand quite as firmly as he does today. But he was so engaging; there was a wonderful brightness and niceness about him. At that point in his career, he wasn't a finished golfer. But he hit the ball very long; he could putt under pressure. And even then, there was an aura about him."

Palmer's 1954 U.S. Amateur Pin; an early addition to what would become an extensive collection of personal golf memorabilia.

After 24 holes, Sweeny had a two-hole lead. Palmer drew even by winning the 25th and 27th, and moved ahead on the 32nd hole, eventually winning the match one up. "That day," he later recalled, "was the turning point in my life. Before then, I'd known I'd always play golf; not as a club pro, but in some other capacity. I guess, in some vague way, I pictured myself as a businessman, competing in all the top amateur tournaments. But winning the national amateur championship gave me the confidence to do what I really wanted to do with my life. Not only was it one of my proudest moments; it led directly to my going out on the tour as a professional golfer. And obviously, that led to everything that came afterward."

On November 15, 1954, Palmer announced his decision to turn pro, and signed a three-year endorsement contract with the Wilson Sporting Goods Company that would pay him just under $5,000 a year. Under the existing PGA regulations, he would be ineligible to win prize money until six months had passed, but was allowed to participate in professional tournaments immediately. His first effort as a pro was the Miami Open, where he failed to survive the 36-hole cut. Meanwhile, between winning his amateur title and starting his pro career, Arnold Palmer had fallen in love.

The object of Palmer's affection was Winifred Walzer, the 20-year-old daughter of a canned-goods-company president who lived in Coopersburg, Pennsylvania. They'd met in September at an amateur tournament. And while "Winnie" was smitten with her suitor, Arnold remembers, "Her parents didn't like the idea of their daughter running off with a young fellow who'd just turned pro and hadn't earned a penny at his new job." Impatient to be wed, the young couple eloped five days before Christmas and was married by a justice of the peace in Falls Church, Virginia. Technically, their union was subject to annulment, since Winnie was underage and parental permission was required. But four decades later, the Palmers are still together despite the myriad pressures of their world.

And what a world it was at the start. Professional golf in 1954 was far different from the pro tour today. It was a vagabond life whose participants were described by *Time* magazine as "a cross between the knights of King Arthur's circular table and a roaming tribe of Arab nomads." Virtually all of the touring pros held second jobs to make ends meet. And as has always been the case, if a golfer didn't perform extraordinarily well in a tournament, he would lose to someone else who did.

Nine days after his marriage, Palmer returned to Miami to compete in the McNaughton Pro-Am.

Because the tournament wasn't an official tour event, he was eligible for prize money and won $900. The next week, under similar circumstances, he earned $1,000 by finishing second in the Panama Open. The first tournament after his six-month "residency" was complete was the Fort Wayne Open, where he placed 25th and earned $145. Meanwhile, as the financial realities of life on the tour took hold, Arnold and Winnie began living in a tow-trailer attached to their 1952 Ford.

Then, in August 1955, Palmer journeyed to Toronto to compete in the Canadian Open. He began with a first-round 64 and followed with rounds of 67, 64, and 70, for his inaugural victory on the pro tour. There was no way of knowing it at the time, but his four-round total of 265 was the lowest he would ever shoot in an official tour event. And in 40 years of professional golf, he would never open a tournament with a round lower than 64.

Palmer entered 31 official events in 1955. His earnings came to $265 per tournament, and his average finish was 22nd place, not counting six tournaments where he withdrew or failed to make the cut. The next year, he entered 30 official events and won twice, with official earnings of $16,145. In 1957, his performance improved markedly with four victories, 17 top-10 finishes, and official earnings of $27,803. Then came 1958, Palmer's breakthrough year highlighted by the Masters in Augusta, Georgia.

Hundreds of professional tournaments are played throughout the world annually, but four carry special distinction – the Masters, U.S. Open, British Open, and PGA. The Masters is an exclusive invitational tournament conducted by the Augusta National Golf Club. The U.S. and British Opens are the championships of the United States Golf Association and the Royal & Ancient Golf Club, the ruling bodies of American and British golf. The PGA is conducted by the Professional Golfers Association, an organization comprised primarily of club pros. These four "major" titles are the most important championships in professional golf. No matter how many tournaments a golfer wins, no matter how much money he makes, he won't be considered "great" unless he has won a "major." And because of the pressure and level of competition involved, it is one of golf's truisms that tournament golf is a very different game from "major" tournament golf.

The Masters heralds the coming of spring, and is the only one of golf's majors played

> *"The first time I saw Arnold Palmer was at a tournament in Tijuana in 1955. My wife said to me, 'I saw the most exciting golfer I've ever seen today; a fellow named Palmer.' I thought she meant Johnny Palmer; a short guy with rosy cheeks and bushy black hair. She said, 'No, this guy looks more like a middleweight fighter.' So I was puzzled, but the next day on the course I saw a young guy with his shirt hanging out, whacking the heck out of the ball, and sometimes it landed in the fairway and sometimes not. And that was Arnold Palmer."*
>
> JIM MURRAY

annually at the same site. The tournament was conceived by Bobby Jones, who as an amateur won the U.S. Open four times, the British Open thrice, and the U.S. Amateur Championship five times. In 1930, at age 28, Jones retired from competitive golf. That same year, he and New York financier Clifford Roberts formed a consortium to buy a 365-acre commercial nursery in Georgia for $70,000. Their goal was to create an exclusive golf club for men, with no swimming pool, no tennis courts, and no women's tees. The club opened in early 1933, with a members tournament commemorating the event. One year later, Jones expanded the tournament, and the Masters was born.

One of the blessings that accompanies a career in golf is going to work in beautiful surroundings. Most golfers consider Augusta National the most beautiful golf course they've ever played. It's said that the sun seems brighter there, the sky bluer, the wind gentler, the pines more stately, and the azaleas more beautiful than on any other golf course in the world. "I don't want to sound overly sentimental about it," Sam Snead once remarked. "But with the course looking the

The Bing Crosby Pro-Am, one of 31 tournaments Palmer entered in 1955.

way it does and the spirit of Bobby Jones running around, sometimes it feels as though the Masters is played on hallowed ground."

Palmer had played in the Masters three times prior to 1958, and placed seventh in 1957. But 1958 saw him primed as never before, having finished second, third, first, and second in four of the five tour events leading up to Augusta. He began the 1958 Masters with rounds of 70, 73, and 68. And after 11 holes of the final round, he was one stroke ahead of the field.

Then, on the par-3 12th hole, Palmer found trouble. His tee shot carried over the green and became embedded when it landed in mud. A rules official was called to the scene and decreed that the ball had to be played as it lay. Palmer did so; moving his ball 18 inches with a wedge. Then he chipped onto the green, and two-putted for a double bogey-5. That apparently dropped him from the lead. But instead of moving to the 13th tee, Palmer returned to the spot where his ball had been embedded, dropped a ball over his shoulder, and replayed the hole. This time, he chipped successfully onto the green and holed his first putt for a par-3.

Arnold Palmer challenges a rules official during the 1958 Masters. It would prove to be the pivotal moment in his first major victory.

What Palmer had done was within his rights. Because of previous heavy rain, the last round of the tournament was being played under a rule that allowed players to lift and drop their ball without penalty if it became embedded in its own pitmark on any part of the course other than a sand trap, water hazard, or putting green. Palmer was fully conversant with the rule. The official who had ruled against him was not.

Several holes later, Palmer's challenge was upheld, and he was retroactively credited with a par-3 for his provisional ball. He finished the tournament with a final-round 73 and a four-round total of 284. Then he waited in the clubhouse while 10 contenders made runs at him and failed. His successful rules challenge had gained him two strokes. And his margin of victory was one.

Palmer won only once more in 1958 – at the Pepsi Open in July. But he performed consistently week in and week out. By year's end, he'd won $42,608, placing him first on the official earnings list. That left him financially secure enough to exchange his tow-trailer for a hotel room on the road. Then he and Winnie bought a three-bedroom house on six acres of land overlooking the home he'd lived in as a boy.

1958 was also the year in which Palmer began a friendship with Dwight Eisenhower, then President of the United States. Legend has it that the two men first played golf together at Augusta the day after Palmer's 1958 Masters triumph. But legends are often inaccurate. In reality, they were introduced five months later at the Laurel Valley Golf Club in Ligonier, Pennsylvania. And Palmer was so unpretentious and quiet that Eisenhower didn't know who he was. Over the years, the two men would develop a fondness similar to a father-and-son relationship. But on October 2, 1958, the chagrined President wrote:

Dear Mr. Palmer,

Because of the general con-fusion the other day, I failed to realize when Ben Fairless (Chairman of the Board of U.S. Steel) introduced us that you were the Arnold Palmer of 1958 Masters fame. I hope you will forgive my lack of reaction and accept, even this belatedly, my warm congratula-tions on your splendid victory.

Ben suggests that some time we might have an opportunity to play at Augusta. This I should very much like though, judging from the brand of golf I have recently been displaying, I would be more than embarrassed.

Sincerely, Dwight D. Eisenhower

In 1959, Palmer's performance slid a notch from the previous year. He won the Thunderbird Invitational with four sub-par rounds totaling 266. But then, after leading the Masters with seven holes to play, he lofted a ball into Rae's Creek for a triple bogey-6, and Art Wall birdied five of the last six holes for a one-stroke triumph over Cary Middlecoff. The following month, Palmer returned to the winner's circle, capturing the Oklahoma City Open. And he won again in the next-to-last tournament of the year, the West Palm Beach Open. Still, his official earn-ings amounted to $10,000 less than in 1958, and he fell from first to fifth place on the offi-cial earnings list.

"I worried about money a lot in those days," Palmer would later admit. "I'd grown up in a steel town in Pennsylvania during the Depression. I'd seen people lose their jobs and their homes. And while I was confident of my ability as a golfer, there was no way I could know with certainty what the future might bring for me and my family."

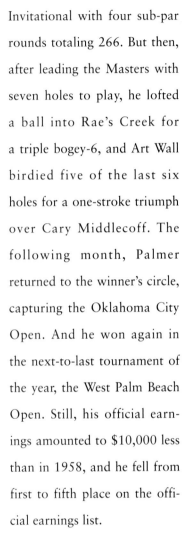

"Arnold has what I call an 'Eisenhower smile.' Those two men, they'd smile and their whole faces would look so pleasant; it was like they were smiling all over."

BYRON NELSON

There was even the possibility that his game had peaked and was about to begin a downward slide. Palmer was a marvelous driver, long and straight. But as Ben Hogan noted, "Arnold's swing might work for him, but no one else should try it." His short iron game was average for a pro. And on the green, he stood over putts in an odd sort of way, pigeon-toed, knock-kneed, his body frozen. Indeed, it seemed to many as though he won despite his game rather than because of it.

Still, at the same time Palmer was questioning his future, the public was starting to take note of his prowess. Part of his appeal was in his looks. So many golfers of that era were pasty-faced, over-weight, skinny, or otherwise constructed in a way that kept them from looking like athletes. But at five feet ten, 175 pounds, with thick biceps and broad shoulders, Arnold Palmer looked like a competitor. Part of his appeal was the way he played. People were used to watching great golfers calculate percentages on the course, coolly and scientifically as though they were playing chess. Palmer, by contrast, went for broke like a weekend golfer whenever there was the slightest bit of daylight. At times he seemed to will his ball into the cup as much as he stroked it in. He almost never left his putts short. Indeed, one fan would later observe that

"Arnie always wanted to turn pro. Forget about anything else you might have heard or read. As far back as I can remember, he knew where he was going. And man, look out! He was going to do it. That's why he's Arnie."

JERRY PALMER

Palmer putted "like a hockey player whacking slapshots past a goalie." But often enough, the ball went in the hole, and the success or failure of every shot was written in emotion on Palmer's face.

In sum, Arnold Palmer was a new type of professional golfer. And he was living in an era that was about to become a "golden age" for golf. The Depression and World War II were over. In the 1950s, the population of the United States had grown by twenty percent, and most of that growth was in the suburbs. For the first time in American history, white-collar workers outnumbered their blue-collar counterparts. Huge sums of money were being invested in real estate. Developers could afford to build, and people could afford to join, private clubs. And the President of the United States was a much-loved man with a nice-guy image and a passion for golf.

But just as important, there was a new spirit in America – one of restless excitement and hope. Americans were ready for new frontiers, new heroes and new challenges. "It was a time," Palmer would later recall, "when the American people were beginning to feel that anything might be accomplished if only we were bold enough to try."

And everything about Arnold Palmer fit so nicely into that.

Palmer, during his rookie season as a pro, February 1955.

It was a time for new challenges and new heroes.

"The American people were beginning to feel that anything might be accomplished if only we were bold enough to try."
ARNOLD PALMER

Above: Perched on the back porch of the Latrobe family home, a three-year-old
Arnold Palmer is joined by his grandparents, Charles and Inez Morrison, and sister, Lo
Below: Arnold, age six, packing a toy six-shooter, poses with Lois Jean.

"When I was in college, I thought about becoming an attorney.
But I wasn't smart enough; I hate being cooped up indoors; and I'm too nice a guy."

ARNOLD PALMER

Although Palmer was interested in many sports as a schoolboy, he would
concentrate on what he did best – play golf. While at Latrobe High, Arnold was a standout
on the school golf team, as seen here with fellow 1946 teammates Ed Matko and Bob Moore.
Even then, Arnold attracted a crowd of admirers.

Howler yearbooks from Arnold's days
as a student at Wake Forest College.

Palmer blasts out of a
bunker at the 1954 USGA
Amateur Championship.

Palmer's signature driver
from the late 1950s,
and the putter and iron
he used during
high school in the 1940s.

"Forty years ago, I was fortunate enough to win the USGA Amateur Championship. That win marked a turning point in my life. It gave me the confidence I needed to pursue a career in golf."
ARNOLD PALMER

A victorious Arnold Palmer after defeating Robert Sweeny (right).

Palmer's golden 1954 USGA Amateur Championship trophy.

Above: Doris Palmer hugs the newly crowned USGA Amateur Champion.
Below: "Deacon" Palmer joins his family as Arnold embraces golf's most prestigious amateur trophy.

Facing page: A jubilant Palmer receives his first green jacket
from 1957 Masters Champion Doug Ford at the 1958 Masters.

"Winnie has always tried to stay out of the limelight. Over the years,
she's declined 10 times as many interviews as she's granted to people who
wanted to talk to Mrs. Arnold Palmer. But she's always been there for Arnold
when he needed her. She was the mainstay in raising two wonderful daughters.

She kept the house and did all the cooking herself. In the early years,
she handled a lot of Arnold's business arrangements. Even today,
she's probably his most trusted advisor, and that's not taking anything away
from Alastair Johnston or Mark McCormack. Personally, professionally,
in every aspect of his life, Winnie has always been there for Arnold."

Doc Giffin

Above: Arnold and Winnie, with their second daughter, Amy, at their home in Latrobe, in August 1958.
Facing page: The newlyweds, on tour at the 1955 Houston Open.

Part Two

THE KING

Sports Illustrated's Grecian Amphora,
awarded to Arnold Palmer,
1960 "Sportsman of the Year."

IN EVERY SPORT, THERE ARE
LANDMARK YEARS WHEN THE GAME IRREVOCABLY

changes. 1927 will be always remembered as the year in which Babe Ruth hit 60 home runs and the New York Yankees were the greatest team ever. In 1958, the Baltimore Colts topped the New York Giants in sudden-death overtime, and pro football found new fans by the millions. In 1979, Magic Johnson and Larry Bird entered the NBA, and pro basketball was never the same again. But no year ever meant more to a sport than 1960 meant to golf, and the man with the magic wand was Arnold Palmer. He elevated his profession to new heights. And as Dan Jenkins later wrote, "For a few years, we absolutely forgot that anyone else played the game."

Palmer's "golden year" began with a 25th-place finish in the Los Angeles Open. He came up a winner in the Palm Springs Desert Classic, but other than that, failed to finish higher than fifth until the eighth tournament of the season. Then, in successive weeks, he won the Texas and Baton Rouge Opens and holed a 32-foot birdie putt on the final hole of the Pensacola Open to edge Doug Sanders by one stroke. "I was awestruck," said Al Geiberger, Palmer's playing partner at Pensacola, who watched him birdie six of the last 10 holes. "You can't do that in golf."

The victory at Pensacola was Palmer's third in a row – the first time since 1952 that anyone on the tour had achieved that feat. But it was only a

Facing page: 1960 heralds golf's new king.

Marching toward victory at the 1960 Masters
with caddie "Iron Man."

prelude to the Masters. Three weeks later, Palmer took the lead at Augusta with a first-round 67. Troubled by a blister on his foot midway through the second round, he put a torn scorecard in his shoe and maintained the lead. After three rounds, he still headed the field. But on the final day, he faltered; and by the time he reached the 17th hole, he trailed Ken Venturi by one stroke.

After his drive on 17, Palmer played an 8-iron to the green, leaving himself a 27-foot birdie putt. He lined it up, but was bothered by spectators jostling for position and stepped back to wait for calm. Then he returned to the ball ... moved away a second time ... came back ... stood over the ball ... and stroked his putt to the lip of the cup where it hung for an instant ... and fell in.

As the putt dropped, Palmer leapt high in the air. Later, he acknowledged, "I couldn't think of anything till I got to the 18th tee. It was just like the day when I bought my first car. I drove it all around town to show it off to everyone. My feet never touched the ground that day either."

On 18, Palmer followed his tee shot with a perfectly placed 6-iron, five feet to the left of the pin. Watching him line up his birdie putt, fellow golfer Bob Rosburg told a reporter, "Arnold will get it in

Palmer seemed to be walking on air after his 27-foot birdie putt dropped on the 71st hole of the 1960 Masters. He would then birdie the final hole to capture his second green jacket.

the hole if he has to stare it in. The ball's scared of him." The roar of the crowd followed. Palmer had won his second Masters. But more important was the way he'd done it, birdieing the last two holes under incredible pressure to win by a single stroke.

The following week, *Sports Illustrated* decreed, "From a wild climax, Arnold Palmer emerged as an authentic and unforgettable hero." *Time* magazine labelled Palmer "the brightest star of a new generation of professionals." And *Life* began its tournament coverage with the headline: "At Masters, Palmer Replaces Hogan, Snead." This time, Dwight Eisenhower did play a round of golf with the Masters champion the day after the tournament. And Palmer appeared on two popular TV programs – "The Perry Como Show" and "Masquerade."

Palmer's next tournament was the Houston Classic, where he tied for first in regulation play but lost in a playoff to Bill Collins. That began a five-week "drought" during which he finished fifth in the Tournament of Champions and third in the Oklahoma City Open. Then he journeyed to Colorado for the U.S. Open at Cherry Hills. And when that tournament was done, the world had a cornerstone on which to build The Palmer Legend to near-mythic proportions.

The U.S. Open heralds the start of summer. It's the most important tournament in golf, and in 1960 it began poorly for Palmer. His first shot landed in a stream to the right of the fairway, and all he could salvage was a double bogey-6. That led to a first-round 72, four strokes behind Mike Souchak. And a second-round 71 left him eight strokes off the pace.

The final two rounds of the Open were played on the same day, known by tradition as "Open Saturday." It had been that way since 1898, and would continue as such until 1965, when the USGA shifted to the more conventional four-day format. Palmer began "Open Saturday" with a morning-round 72 that left him in 15th place, well behind established pros like Ben Hogan, Sam Snead, and Julius Boros. By any rational calculation, he was now out of contention. And Bob Drum, who had covered Palmer's career for the *Pittsburgh Press* since Arnold was 16 years old, told him so.

Drum's remarks came in the clubhouse during lunch. Palmer was talking about the par-4, 346-yard first hole. It bothered him that he hadn't been able to reach the green with his tee shot in any of the first three rounds. "It really makes me hot," he said. "If I drive that green, I could shoot a hell of a score. I might even shoot a 65. What'll that do?"

The U.S. Open's prestigious prize, awarded to Palmer after his phenomenal final round 65 at Cherry Hills.

"Nothing," Drum told him. "You're too far back."

"Well, it would give me a 280. Doesn't 280 always win the Open?"

At 1:45 p.m., Palmer began his final round, seven strokes off the pace. On the first hole, he drove the green. And then he followed with seven of the most remarkable holes ever played in tournament golf.

- No.1 Par-4: Two putts for a birdie.
- No.2 Par-4: 35-foot putt from the fringe of the green; birdie.
- No.3 Par-4: Approach shot to within a foot of the hole; birdie.
- No.4 Par-4: 18-foot putt; birdie.
- No.5 Par-5: Recovered from a tee shot in the rough; par.
- No.6 Par-3: 25-foot putt; birdie.
- No.7 Par-4: Wedge shot to within six feet of the hole; birdie.

Now the U.S. Open was in chaos, with golf's greatest names trading places on the leaderboard. At 2:45 p.m., Mike Souchak held the lead at five under par; one stroke ahead of Julius Boros, Dow Finsterwald, and a 20-year-old amateur named Jack Nicklaus. Ben Hogan was three under; one stroke ahead of Jack Fleck, Jerry Barber, and Palmer. A few minutes before 4:00 p.m., Souchak fell into a three-way tie for first. Then he bogeyed the ninth hole, and Nicklaus got hot to lead the field. At 4:15 p.m., on the 13th hole, Nicklaus three-putted from 10 feet, and fell into a

In dramatic, come-from-behind fashion, Palmer cards a final-round 65
to win his second "major" of 1960 – the U.S. Open.

four-way tie with Palmer, Boros, and Fleck. At 4:45 p.m., Palmer, Fleck, and Ben Hogan shared the lead. Then Fleck's putting soured.

Finally, at 5:30 p.m., Palmer and Hogan stood alone. It was as dramatic a moment as golf has ever seen. Ben Hogan, in the twilight of his career, desperately seeking a fifth Open crown. Arnold Palmer, the heir apparent, striving to ascend the throne. And on the par-5 17th hole, it was Hogan who faltered. Gambling for a birdie, he went directly for the flag on his third shot instead of playing safely away from a pond in front of the green. In the history of golf, no one ever hit more shots with near-total accuracy and control than Ben Hogan. But this time he failed. His pitch fell short, hitting near the top of the bank and spinning back into the water. All he could salvage was a bogey-6, followed by a triple bogey-7 on the final hole.

A triumphant Palmer hurls his visor in the air to celebrate his U.S. Open victory.

Now Palmer was alone, playing the last two holes in par for a 280 total and the 1960 U.S. Open crown. But more impressive than the fact that he'd won was the manner in which his victory had been achieved. Once again, he'd come from behind with what was fast becoming his trademark "charge." His final-round 65 was, at the time, the lowest ever for a U.S. Open champion. And he had become only the third man in history to win the Masters and U.S. Open in the same year.

Later, historians would look back on the 1960 Open as the moment when three eras and three remarkable careers collided. There, in full view for everyone to see, was the end of Hogan, the arrival of Nicklaus, and the coronation of Palmer. But to the public, it seemed as though only Arnold Palmer really mattered. And taking flight on the wings of his latest triumph, The Palmer Phenomenon burgeoned to extraordinary proportions.

The reasons for Palmer's popularity were many. First, he was an immensely likable man with an enormous amount of natural warmth and friendliness. He didn't have to work at getting along with anyone; it was instinctive. People liked Arnold because they sensed he liked them. He genuinely enjoyed shaking hands, bantering with the gallery, and making people feel good. He was a common man in the best sense of the word; uncomplicated, stable, one of the guys. When he had a drink, he did it in public. When he smoked, it was on the golf course for everyone to see. When he hit a shot, good or bad, he reacted the way a normal person

"I like to think that, the next time the U.S. Open is at Cherry Hills, some young golfer will tee up for the first hole and say to himself, 'This is where Arnold Palmer drove the green that day in 1960 when he shot his final-round 65.'"

ARNOLD PALMER

"*A lot of people think Arnold won as many tournaments as he did because of his aggressiveness. I personally think he would have won more if he hadn't been so bold. Sure, he won some tournaments by being aggressive but, in my view, it cost him more than it won for him.*"

LEE TREVINO

would. At times, he seemed almost innocent, walking down the fairway tugging at his pants, which always seemed to be sliding down. "He's totally inelegant; a representative of the masses," Oleg Cassini once sniffed. "If his pants fit, he wouldn't have to hitch them up all the time." But except for Cassini, no one seemed to care. In Palmer's world, fashion was far less important than whether or not a man replaced his divots.

Then there was the quality of Palmer's game. His bold style of play, his ability to perform under pressure, and the frequency with which he came from behind all mirrored and reinforced the image of his personality. Arnold Palmer approached a golf ball the way Ted Williams stepped into the batter's box and Joe Louis entered a prize ring. He didn't just play a course; he attacked each hole as though intent on obliterating par. Spectators couldn't turn away for an instant because at any moment – BOOM – something might happen.

Golfers are supposed to win tournaments by avoiding mistakes. But Palmer seemed to win by making mistakes and then overcoming them. At times, he acted as though there wasn't a golf shot he didn't think he could hit perfectly. He tried shots that most professional golfers would never attempt. And if a shot hit a tree or bounced off a rock, not only did he know the next one would work; he knew it would make up for what had gone wrong on his previous swing.

"Every time Arnold drives, it looks like he's trying to hole his tee shot," Sam Snead told a reporter. Charlie Sifford proclaimed, "Arnold Palmer is the most aggressive player in the history of golf. Some guys, if they're behind six or seven strokes, they start playing for fourth place. Arnold could be behind six or seven strokes, and the last day he'd go out and try to shoot zero." "When Arnold stands over a 20-foot putt," said Dow Finsterwald, his best friend on the tour, "he acts as though he expects to make it, which I suppose is the way we all ought to think."

"I asked Arnold once whether he ever prayed during a tournament," fellow pro Dave Marr remembers. "And he told me, 'No; all I ever ask is that I'm healthy when I get there. I'll take care of the rest.'"

Palmer on the golf course was perpetual drama, radiating the intensity of a great performer. "There were so many times," British writer Hugh McIlvanney remembers, "when Arnold appeared to be considering the alternatives; whether to go over the water for the green, or lay up short with an iron. And you knew in the end he'd go for the green, but there was that marvelous dramatic sense about him. He'd brood and stalk, and then there'd be a great roar from the crowd, because Arnold had reached for a wood and, caution be damned, he was going to carry the water."

Palmer's game was such a roller-coaster ride of bold shots, heroic saves, falling back, and coming from behind that he himself once felt compelled to protest, "Believe me; I don't do it deliberately. Nobody in his right mind would want to live so dangerously." But when pressed on the subjects of "boldness" and "trouble," he would discourse in the manner of a script written for John Wayne:

• "When I take a shot that seems bold, it never occurs to me that I might miss it. And when I do, I'm surprised as hell. I can't believe it."

• "You've got to learn to live with trouble, and you've got to learn how to get out of it. It's a

"The only really unplayable lie I can think of is when you're supposed to be playing golf and come home with lipstick on your collar."

ARNOLD PALMER

little like bleeding. Your first objective is to get it stopped. Then you try to heal it. You tell yourself there's nothing here you haven't faced before; and if you've done it once, you can do it again."

• "I don't look on it as a gamble, really. I just look on it as a harder shot. Why hit a conservative shot? When you miss it, you're in just as much trouble as when you miss a bold one."

• "Trouble is bad to get into but fun to get out of. If you're in trouble, eighty percent of the time there's a way out. If you can see the ball, you can probably hit it; and if you can hit it, you can move it; and if you can move it, you might be able to knock it into the hole. At least, it's fun to try."

• "I suppose there's a place to play it safe. But as far as I'm concerned, it's not on the golf course."

Arnold Palmer projected to his fans like a man who would eschew the blindfold at his own firing squad. He was even licensed to fly an airplane, which added to his aura. And his image was further burnished by a remarkable affinity for the press.

By and large, golfers enjoy a "sweetheart" media. One reason for that is, there's less feuding and controversy to write about in golf than in other sports. Also, there's a tradition that golf is a "gentleman's sport" and should be covered as such. The scope of the game further demands a symbiotic relationship between media and performer. When a reporter covers baseball, football, basketball, or any other major sport, the contest occurs in one place. But a golf tournament unfolds over a vast expanse with dozens of players performing simultaneously, and it's impossible for one person to see everything that happens. Thus, reporters are dependent upon the golfers themselves to supply the details that fill out their stories.

Moreover, in golf, there's a subtle system of carrots and sticks that helps keep the media in check. Golf writers come to a tournament and receive free shirts, free pants, and free golf equipment. They get low room rates, complimentary playing privileges and gratis $50 dinners. They're invited to cocktail parties and hosted throughout the tournament in a very genteel manner. "But if you rip someone or make fun of their tournament," warns Rick Reilly of *Sports Illustrated*, "they're pissed off at you forever. And no one wants to slay a goose that's laying golden eggs."

Thus, Palmer was working within a friendly environment to begin with. And beyond that, he

"If it wasn't for flying, I wouldn't be playing golf today. I loathe driving 2,000 miles every Monday morning."

ARNOLD PALMER

was perfectly constituted for dealing with the media. He had an innate sense of publicity and what the press could do for him. Indeed, Ray Cave, at one time a writer with *Sports Illustrated*, recalls Arnold heeding his advice as to what color shirt he should wear on the last day of the Masters so he'd stand out on the cover of the magazine if he won.

"I never had any trouble dealing with Arnold, and I don't think anyone else did either," recalls Jerry Izenberg of the *Newark Star-Ledger*. "He was likable; he was colorful; he was always accessible. And when someone is that accessible to the press, it means one of two things – either he's a nice guy or he's a manipulator. And I never heard anyone suggest that Arnold Palmer was a manipulator." Sportswriter Jim Murray is equally expansive, adding, "There are athletes you work with, and no matter how nice they are to you, you know they're difficult with other people, whether it's other writers, photographers, fans, whatever. But Arnold Palmer is one of the few people in sports who I've never heard anyone say anything bad about. He was perfect for our business."

By the summer of 1960, Palmer's popularity was so great that newspapers and magazines were giving extra coverage to golf. Reporters were told to place his name high in stories, regardless of how he fared in a tournament. And in addition to everything else, one more extraordinarily important force was at work – television. In 1950, only eight percent of American families owned a TV set. But by 1960, that number was eighty-eight percent, and TV was at the heart of American life. John Kennedy won the 1960 presidential election in part because he looked more presidential than Richard Nixon in their televised debates. American culture was being transformed by Ed Sullivan, Walt Disney and "Gunsmoke." Four decades earlier, Babe Ruth, Jack Dempsey, Red Grange and Bill Tilden had presided over a "golden age" of sports. Now, thanks to TV, new legends were being born. The entire nation was able to see the Olympics, "Wide World of Sports," Mantle versus Maris and the Boston Celtics.

Golf had been televised on a sporadic basis as early as 1953, but few sports translated more poorly onto a small black-and-white screen. TV simply failed to transmit what a golf course looked like or the sensation of a tiny ball in flight. But Palmer was different from any golfer before him. Not only was he photogenic; he was telegenic. TV was the perfect medium for him. And as a result of his ascent, the

By 1960, it must have seemed to Palmer as though "Arnie's Army" was everywhere.

TV cameras no longer had to focus on 50 ordinary-looking men walking around hitting balls that viewers couldn't see. There was one main man to cover; one superstar; one hero. "It was a classic case of the right man being in the right place at the right time," Jack Nicklaus later acknowledged. And when Palmer won the 1960 Masters and U.S. Open, both with dramatic come-from-behind finishes, the genie was out of the bottle, never to be put back again. Television magnified everything. And now, in the age of television, viewers were about to witness one of the most remarkable love affairs in sports history – the phenomenon known as "Arnie's Army."

Ben Hogan once remarked. "I don't know why anyone would go to a golf tournament. The prices are inflated; they don't let you in the clubhouse; and you can't see a thing." Still, people do go to tournaments, although before Palmer the galleries were comprised largely of country-club types and the limousine-executive crowd. Most often, they followed whichever golfer was in the lead or they sat by the 18th hole. Then, after Palmer's victory at Cherry Hills, golf witnessed a grassroots revolution unlike anything seen before. People who had never been near a golf course in their life started coming out in droves. They followed wherever Palmer went, and the face of golf was forever changed.

There have always been fanatical spectators at sports events. But golf, as opposed to baseball or college football, had never seen anything like "Arnie's Army" before. It was the exception to every rule that had ever existed on a golf course. These were noisy people. They roamed all over the place, leaving garbage behind, shouting, "Go get 'em, Arnie" and "Charge!" There were even times when Palmer would mishit a ball into the crowd surrounding the green, and someone would kick it back out toward the hole for him. That's how much Arnold's enlistees loved their general. They'd even cheat for him.

"After a while," photographer Walter Iooss recalls, "Arnold needed state troopers just to move him through the crowds. And believe me, no other golfer in those days needed state troopers." "Trying to follow Palmer down the course," George Plimpton later said, "was not unlike running before the bulls at Pamplona." No one on the course needed a leaderboard to know how Arnold was doing. It was evident from the groans and roars that emanated from his followers.

Asked why his fans were so devoted to him, Palmer quipped, "Maybe it's because I'm in the rough so much that I get to know them all personally." But obviously, more was involved. Before Palmer made his mark, a lot of golfers acted as though spectators were intruding on their private world. And now, here was the greatest golfer on earth, involving thousands of people in his work. People identified with Arnold and viewed him as the man they'd like to be. If he was walking down the fairway and someone in the gallery shouted to him, often he shouted back; sometimes "thank you," sometimes a more elaborate response. Every duffer knows how it feels to hit a ball into water. If Palmer's shot wound up in a lake, he might turn to the gallery and announce, "I sure blew that one, didn't I?"

"We can't play his game, but he plays ours," British columnist Peter Andrews wrote. And almost magically, Palmer's fans joined by the thousands to form "the world's largest private army." "People see themselves winning through Palmer," explained Ernest Dichter, a psychologist who analyzed the phenomenon for the *Wall Street Journal*. "He looks and acts like a regular guy, and at the same time he does things others only wish they could do. His expressiveness makes spectators feel they're part of his game. He looks as though he needs their help, and they respond."

> *"Arnold embarrassed a lot of guys on the tour into signing autographs. A lot of players used to snub fans. They'd give some kind of excuse about being busy and run on, and Arnold was so wonderful about it, so patient with fans, that the other guys had no choice but to follow his example."*
>
> DOW FINSTERWALD

The larger Arnie's Army grew, the more Palmer wanted to succeed in its eyes. "This might sound corny," he said later, "but I tried to look the whole gallery in the eye. Maybe it was a selfish thing on my part, but I liked seeing the happiness my golf seemed to give them." To many, it became a status symbol just to be part of Arnie's Army. His troops felt they were participants in one of sport's greatest dramas. Palmer himself used the crowds for motivation, and there were other advantages as well. When a large crowd presses against a fairway or green, it outlines the target for a golfer. Also, many pros will shade their shots in the direction of a crowd, because if the shot goes off line, the crowd's presence will keep it from bouncing too far. For most golfers, this "human wall" is available only on the 18th green. But Palmer brought his wall with him to virtually every hole.

"I liked playing in front of the Army," Dave Marr remembers. "It was wild at times. When Arnold teed up his ball, they cheered. And if I'd walked on water, they wouldn't have noticed. But I enjoyed the excitement of all those people, and I think the Army was good for golf."

However, others took a contrary view. "I dread every round I play with Palmer," complained Frank Beard. "It's got nothing to do with Arnie personally. Arnie's easy to play with, but Arnie's Army is impossible. They run and stampede to see Arnie. They knock you down. They know nothing about golf etiquette, and have no regard for anyone who's playing with Palmer. They're not real golf fans. They just look at the paper and say, 'Hey, Arnie's in town; let's go see Arnie.' They don't understand the game at all. They wouldn't appreciate it if he did the greatest thing in the world. If Arnie pees in the fairway, they're happy."

"They don't know anybody's here but Palmer," Jerry Barber said of the crowds. And Gary Player added in wonder, "You know, if Arnold turned and said to the gallery, 'All of you go down and jump in the river,' they'd do it." But the impact of Arnie's Army was undeniable. Perhaps Dave Kindred of the *Atlanta Constitution* summed it up best when he wrote: "Bobby Jones made a golf course a cathedral. Palmer makes it a sports arena."

After his victory in the 1960 U.S. Open, Palmer faced his next significant challenge in Scotland. The occasion was the British Open – a "major" championship by tradition, but one that had fallen on hard times. Most of the world's best players avoided the event, because to enter they were required to play in a 36-hole qualifying

"I try to be friendly; I give a thousand percent to the public when I'm on a golf course. But when I'm off the course, I like my privacy, and I like it more than most people. I stay in my hotel room; I order from room service; I'm like a hermit. If no one recognizes me, I feel wonderful. Arnold is different. He absolutely loves being around people."

LEE TREVINO

The General and his Army.

tournament. And even if they were successful, the prize money was minimal. "I played the British Open in 1937," Byron Nelson recalls. "It took a week to get there and a week to get home. I was the low American; finished fourth or fifth. And what it came down to was, I lost a good part of my summer, won $185, and spent $1,000 on boat fare alone."

But Palmer wanted to play in the British Open. Scotland was the cradle of golf. And one of his goals was to be regarded as the best golfer in the world, which to him meant winning the open championship of every country where golf was a major sport. Moreover, he'd just won the Masters and U.S. Open, and was excited by the possibility of becoming the first golfer in history to win all four professional majors in the same year.

Thus, in July, Palmer traveled to St. Andrews in pursuit of the British Open crown. He began the tournament with rounds of 70, 71, and 70, for a three-round total of 211. On the final day, with six holes left, he trailed Kel Nagle by four strokes. Then the Palmer "charge" began. But it wasn't enough. His final-round 68 fell one stroke short, good only for second place.

Palmer with lifelong British Open caddie Tip Anderson at St. Andrews, 1960.

Soon, though, Palmer was winning again; first in a playoff at the Insurance City Open; next at the Mobile Open; and after that, teaming with Sam Snead to capture the Canada Cup. By year's end, he'd won $75,263 to shatter golf's single-season earnings record. But more important, he'd emerged victorious in eight tournaments, finished in the top five in 19 out of 29 tournaments entered, and become the most popular athlete in America. *Sports Illustrated* named him "Sportsman of the Year." And a poll of sportswriters awarded him the prestigious Hickok Belt as "Professional Athlete of the Year."

In the first tournament of 1961, the accolades were followed by what could have been interpreted as an ominous portent. In the opening round of the Los Angeles Open, Palmer was at two under par. Then, on the par-5 18th hole, he decided to "go for broke." But instead of reaching the green in two as planned, he knocked his ball out of bounds four times in succession, took 10 strokes to get within putting range, and scored a horrifying heptagonal-bogey. Asked by reporters how he'd managed to shoot 12 on a single hole, he responded, "It was easy; I missed a 30-foot putt for 11." But the next week, he rebounded to win the San Diego Open. And the following month, he won back-to-back tournaments in Phoenix and Baton Rouge.

That set the stage for the 1961 Masters. And once again, it seemed as though Palmer owned the Augusta National Golf Club. His first-round 68 was good for the lead, and he kept it with a 69 on Friday. That meant he'd been in first place after each of six consecutive rounds over two years at Augusta. But on Saturday, he faltered with a one-over-par 73, and Gary Player moved four strokes ahead of the field. Sunday was washed out by a violent storm. Then, on Monday, Palmer "charged."

"I have a very uncomfortable feeling when Arnold is behind me, breathing down my neck," Gary Player once said. "I'd rather be a stroke behind him than a stroke ahead, and I think that's the feeling of just about everybody on the tour." On Monday, Player got his wish, but not exactly as planned. Plagued by inconsistency, he finished with a two-over-par 74. Meanwhile, Palmer was three under for the day and came to the final hole one stroke in the lead, needing only a par-4 to become the first man in history to win consecutive Masters championships.

"And I blew it," Palmer remembers. "My tee shot was fine; a good drive slightly left on the fairway. The pin was left front, and all I needed

The prestigious Hickok Belt was presented to Arnold Palmer as "Professional Athlete of the Year" in 1960.

on my second shot was a simple 7-iron to the green. It was a shot I'd made a thousand times before. And you know the rest."

Over the years, Palmer has explained the debacle that followed many times:

• "I remember standing there, thinking that all I needed was a four to win; just get it up there on the green and down in two putts. That's where I made my mistake; thinking about something besides hitting the ball. If I'd kept my mind on swinging the club properly, there wouldn't have been any problem."

• "I just went to sleep on that shot. Looking back, I suspect I lifted my head a little early and didn't hit all the way through on it."

• "It was a perfectly easy shot, but I came up off it a little when I hit and pushed it into that bunker on the right. If it had just been a couple of inches more to the left, it wouldn't have rolled the way it did."

But it did roll. And trying to hit out of the bunker, Palmer compounded his initial mistake with one that was worse. "Instead of taking a moment to cool down and study the shot," he remembers, "I went up to it, hurrying to get my win. I figured I could blast out near the cup, and get the ball down with one putt."

This time, though, Palmer's boldness cost him. Exploding out of the sand, he bounced his

"Sometimes I replay shots in my head. Not whole rounds; but yes, I replay key shots occasionally.
Sometimes they're good, and sometimes they're bad. The last hole of the 1961 Masters;
hitting out of the stump at Brookline; shots like that."

ARNOLD PALMER

Palmer double bogeys the last hole at the 1961 Masters.

ball past the hole, off the green, and down a slope toward a nearby television tower. Now he needed to get down in two simply to tie for the lead, but his fourth shot overran the hole by 15 feet. The putt back was probably as difficult a shot as any golfer has ever faced. Palmer rolled it toward the cup and grimaced as it went right. The miracle worker had come up empty, double bogeying the final hole of the 1961 Masters to lose by a stroke.

The loss at Augusta was Palmer's first major collapse since he'd become a national phenomenon. But rather than hold it against him, the public seemed to love him even more. If anything, "Arnie" was now even more like them. And two weeks later, he won again; this time at the Texas Open. At the U.S. Open, he started poorly with rounds of 74 and 75 and had to settle for 12th place despite closing with back-to-back 70s. Then he returned to Scotland for some unfinished business at the British Open, and The Palmer Legend soared to new heights.

"It is doubtful that there was a man present at Birkdale who wanted Palmer to lose," Henry Longhurst wrote when the tournament was done. "It's impossible to overpraise the tact and charm with which this American has conducted himself on his two visits to Britain. He has no fancy airs or graces; he wears no fancy clothes; he makes no fancy speeches. He simply says and does exactly the right thing at the right time, and that is enough."

Longhurst might have added that, on occasion, Palmer also seemed to do the impossible. On the 16th hole of the last round, his third shot landed right of the green in a bush. "The longer I studied it, the worse it looked," Palmer later acknowledged. "But then I walked up on the green, and the first thing that struck me was I could see the ball. That meant there had to be an avenue for escape, so I took my sand wedge and laid it wide open."

Palmer's shot rose high in the air and came to rest two feet from the cup. The subsequent putt gave him a par-5 for the hole, and he won the British Open by a single stroke. Back in the United States, he triumphed again, this time at the Western Open. And he finished the year with six top-five finishes in his final eight starts. That led into 1962, which he began with justifiable confidence. In February, he won back-to-back tournaments for the third time in his career,

Arnold Palmer, runnerup, congratulates first-time Masters champion Gary Player, 1961.

emerging victorious in the Palm Springs Classic and Phoenix Open, the latter victory by 12 strokes. Then he journeyed to Augusta in an attempt to make amends for his double bogey-6 on the previous year's final hole.

It was a memorable Masters, showcasing the best and worst of Arnold Palmer. For three days, he played superb golf, with rounds of 70, 66, and 69, for a two-stroke lead heading into Sunday's action. Then his game fell apart. On the first hole of the final round, he missed an ordinary putt for par. On the second, he missed a 20-inch effort. On three, he drove into the woods. And on four, his tee shot died after 125 yards. He finished the front-nine with a dreadful 39, and lost two more strokes with a double bogey-6 on 10. After 15 holes, he was two strokes behind Gary Player and Dow Finsterwald, and his tee shot on the par-3 16th hole missed the green.

Bobby Jones congratulates Palmer on his third Masters victory in 1962.

But then, again, Palmer "charged." First, he chipped in from 45 feet for a birdie that brought him to within a stroke of the lead. And on 17, he one-putted for another birdie to draw even on the leaderboard. "I never admired anyone in my whole life the way I admired Arnold during those last few holes," Dave Marr said afterward. "I don't know how he did it. You can't imagine how it feels to have a chance at the money and blow it and to pull yourself together after something like that. I asked him how he had the nerve to try that chip shot on 16, and all he told me was he thought the course owed him one."

Palmer's heroics, coupled with the steady play of Finsterwald and Player, set up the first three-way playoff in the history of the Masters. As he had the day before, Arnold started the extra round poorly, and trailed by three strokes at the halfway mark. But then his game caught fire again, and he birdied four of the next five holes to move from three strokes back to a lead of four. He finished with a four-under-par 68, while Finsterwald lost his putting touch and fell to 77. Player fought valiantly, but could do no better than a one-under-par 71.

"I was lucky this year," Palmer said of his third Masters triumph. But clearly more than luck was involved. In the wake of Augusta, Alfred Wright of *Sports Illustrated* wrote, "Palmer's game is composed of human failings that let him fall seemingly hopelessly far behind, and of superhuman resources that enable him to come fighting back as no golfer ever has before."

Gene Sarazen decreed, "This young man has more determination than any player I've ever known. He has only one thing in mind – win, win, win." And Bobby Jones opined, "He's good with all the clubs, but he's got that ability to hole the important putts more than anyone I've ever seen. It's just something in his makeup. Some people play better under pressure and some play worse. He's one who plays better. He's just got it."

Meanwhile, the Palmer bandwagon rolled on. After a fifth-place finish at the Greensboro Open, he won the Texas Open by birdieing three of the last four holes. One week after that, he captured the Tournament of Champions with a 25-foot putt on the final hole. And then he journeyed to Fort Worth for the Colonial National Invitational. For seven years, the Colonial had been a source of aggravation to Palmer. His average finish there had been 23rd place, and the 312 he'd scored in Fort Worth in 1955 was the worst four-round total of his pro career. "I would have just as soon passed the Colonial up this year," Palmer said when the tournament was over. "But it kind of bugged me the way they said I couldn't play the Colonial." So Palmer showed he could play the Colonial with a four-stroke playoff victory over Johnny Pott. It was the second time in his career that he'd won three tournaments in a row. And to complete the

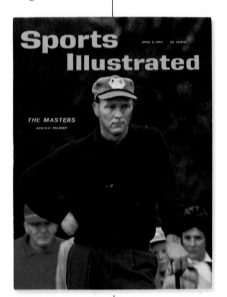

picture, there was one moment during the playoff at the Colonial that confirmed Palmer's best angels to the world.

It happened while Palmer was on the ninth hole, readying to chip from off the green. A young boy was talking to his mother. Palmer was distracted, and turned toward the child. Then he stepped away from his ball, waited for silence, and addressed the ball again. This time, there was a muffled sound as the woman held a hand over her son's mouth to suppress his incipient scream. At that point, a lot of golfers would have ordered security to remove the child. But Palmer simply walked over, patted the boy on the head, and told his mother, "Hey, don't choke him. It's not all that important."

Now even the most hardened skeptics were forced to acknowledge that they'd never seen a phenomenon like Arnold Palmer. In seven years on the tour, he'd won 32 national tournaments in addition to the British, Panama, and Colombia Opens. To the media, the story line of every tournament he entered was his triumph when he won and his tragedy when he lost. His success had become an expected part of golf, like bunkers along the fairway or the flag on each green. To the public, he'd become "something of a worldwide sporting Beatle." And Dan Jenkins, who coined that phrase, observed that things had gotten to the point where it seemed as though, "If Palmer doesn't win your golf tournament, it hasn't been a success."

"The presence of Palmer," Alfred Wright wrote, "hovers over the other tournament pros these days with the same cheerfulness as a mushroom cloud. When they're going well, they not only have to worry about the course; there's always the threat of the famed Palmer 'charge' in the closing round to rob them of their victory." And Palmer's fellow pros seemed almost in awe of him:

Jerry Barber – "Arnold goes right for the throat of the course, and then he shakes it to death."

Doug Sanders – "Playing in a golf tournament with Arnold is like riding a lion down the road, whipping him with a rattlesnake, while trying to get away from a mean guy behind you."

Byron Nelson – "If I had to stake the family jewels on a single eight-foot putt, I'd want Palmer to putt it for me. He exerts so much physical and mental force, it's almost as though he commands the ball to obey him."

Gary Player – "I've been trying to tell myself for too long that it's luck. But now I'm convinced; it's more than luck. Arnie is simply the greatest there ever was. No one has done what this man has done."

No one will ever conquer golf, but Palmer seemed to be coming close. The pro tour had been all but broken up into two divisions – Arnold and everybody else. Palmer remained modest about his achievements. "The whole story," he told a reporter for *Time* magazine, "is that I like to play golf." Meanwhile, in a profile for *The New Yorker*, Herbert Warren Wind, the most respected golf writer in America and a man not given to hyperbole, wrote:

"Arnold Palmer is no less than the most exciting athlete since Babe Ruth. His ability to perform wonders is based on an honest conviction that they are not wonders at all. He wins most often with the kind of finish that most men are lucky to pull off once in a lifetime. The regularity with which he picks up birdies when he has to tends to give the impression that a birdie is almost as accessible as par. No man can go on doing this sort of thing indefinitely. Golf isn't that simple a game. But Palmer has succeeded so often before, that an almost tangible aura of inevitability now suffuses his exploits."

The powers that be were coming close to turning Palmer into a god. And then Jack Nicklaus arrived on the scene.

"Arnold Palmer invented pro golf as it exists today. Ben Hogan didn't make golf popular. Hogan was as much fun to cuddle up to as a porcupine. Nicklaus didn't do it. It was all going on the tour by the time Nicklaus got there. Palmer's the King. He's the one who made it all possible."

RICK REILLY

Hit it hard,
go find it,
hit it hard
"The game of golf consists in hitting a ball over a stretch of country with clubs which have been designed to suit the different positions in which the ball may be found. The charm of the game lies in the wide variety of demands placed on the golfer as his ball progresses."
ENCYCLOPEDIA BRITANNICA
again.

"A long drive is good for the ego."

ARNOLD PALMER

Facing page: Palmer would sink this short, side-hill putt on the final hole
at Augusta to claim his second Masters Championship in 1960.

"A golfer can't dictate what his opponents shoot. He can't wave his arms or tackle a playing partner who's getting ready to putt. But he can always reach within himself to bring out the best in his battle against the laws of physics and par."
ARNOLD PALMER

Palmer on the green at the 1961 British Open.

The oldest trophy in golf. This silver claret jug has been presented to the winner of the British Open since 1872. Palmer received it twice – in 1961 and 1962.

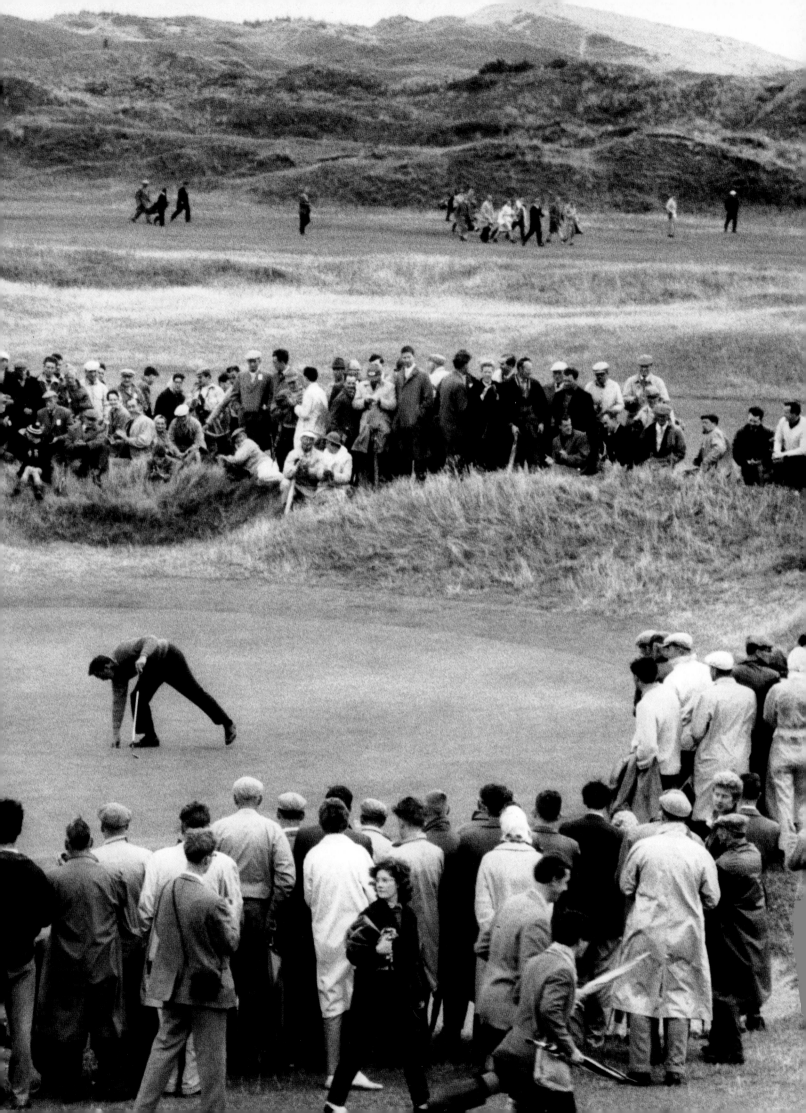

"Being able to play in a beautiful setting is part of the essence of golf. When I'm on a course, I might be in the middle of one of the largest cities in the world with a six-lane super-highway nearby, but I have no sense of that. Instead, I'm in lovely surroundings and that natural beauty is important to me."
Arnold Palmer

Palmer, seen through the azaleas en route to his third Masters championship.

Palmer was the PGA Tour's leading money winner in 1958, 1960, 1962 and 1963.

"There's a tale that's told, presumably apocryphal, about a round of golf that
Arnold Palmer and Ben Hogan played in 1960. On the first hole, Hogan scored a textbook par-3.
Palmer's drive came to rest in a tree stump; his second shot made it to the edge of the green;
and he holed a 40-foot putt for par. On the second hole, Hogan's drive split the fairway;
his second shot was on the green; and he two-putted for another classic par.

Palmer's tee shot landed in three inches of water; he blasted his second shot out onto
the fairway; his third shot came to rest several feet beyond the green; and he chipped in for par.
On the third hole, Hogan executed four more near-perfect precise shots for his third par in
a row. Meanwhile, Palmer's tee shot landed in the rough; his second shot landed in a bunker;
and his third shot bounced into the hole for a birdie. Whereupon Hogan turned to Arnold
and demanded, 'Look, dammit; we're here to play golf. Stop fooling around.'"

JERRY IZENBERG

"*On a golf course, there's nobody else who looks like Palmer. He's got all kinds of distinctive movements; the way he hitches up his pants; the way he hovers over putts, all hunched up. And from my perspective, that's good, because you can't draw golfers the way you draw other athletes. Put John Elway in a Denver Broncos uniform with the number "7" on his chest, give him a face mask, get the throwing gesture right, and you're all set. But golfers dress like a regular guy walking into a supermarket, so everything extra helps. And I'll tell you something else about the Palmer look. If you didn't know anything at all about Arnold Palmer and were just watching him walk by, you'd sense that this is a guy who can handle anything.*"

LEROY NEIMAN

Palmer was followed by crowds the likes of which golf had never seen before.

Palmer's World Series of Golf belt buckle.

*"When we were growing up, Daddy didn't really talk to Peg and me
about golf other than to say, 'This is my job, and this is why I work so hard.'
Certainly, he never pressured us to play. My grandfather tried to get
us to play; he gave us some lessons. But I guess we'd had enough of golf,
watching Daddy and attending tournaments, because to be honest,
neither one of us had any interest in playing."*

AMY PALMER SAUNDERS

"I was independent, and my dad was a disciplinarian. If he said, 'Be home by eleven o'clock,'
two minutes after eleven wasn't good enough. I mean, we're talking Robert Duvall, the Great Santini.
And there were times when I saw him as a very threatening physical person. He never hurt us. I'm not
saying that. He used to spank us with a hair brush, but that's what parents did in those days.
He never ever physically abused us, but there was a lot of yelling about things.

Then I went away to school. My dad hated the idea. It was against everything he believed in.
But my mother worked on Daddy pretty hard, and by the time it got to me it was a done deal,
so I went away for my last two years of high school. And when I came back on vacations,
in addition to fighting with my dad about everything we'd fought about before, I fought with him
about all the issues that kids fight about with their parents when they become self-righteous and think
they know everything there is to know about life. There were no blacks in Latrobe, and I'd argue with
my father about black people. I'd argue with him about women's issues. He couldn't believe I had the
audacity to suggest that his views were unacceptable to me. We were in each other's face a lot. But my
mother didn't seem to mind the way he was all that much. And now, I'm more understanding with
regard to how men of that generation treated women, and the fact that most women of that generation
didn't think they had a choice. I realize it was as much a social phenomenon as an individual thing,
and I respect the way they worked things out between them."

PEG PALMER WEARS

Winnie Palmer at home in Latrobe.

"I'd hate to see golf do what other sports have done. I don't want the game to change. In fact, I'll go further and say that one very important reason for golf's success over the years is that the basic game hasn't changed."
ARNOLD PALMER

Palmer in his Latrobe workshop; the never-ending quest for the perfect club.

This hole-filled driver was one of Palmer's early modifications, intended to reduce air resistance.

"When Amy and I were growing up, my dad didn't have a lot of time for us. He wasn't around all that much, and when he was, most of the action revolved around him. But I never doubted for a minute that he really loved my sister and me. He was always all touchy and huggy. He's real emotional that way, and that was great when I was a kid.

I remember, one time when we were young, he and my mom took us to visit some incredibly wealthy friends of theirs. These people were rich beyond anything we'd ever dreamed of; a huge mansion, all sorts of possessions, live-in nannies and maids. And when dinnertime came, the kids didn't eat with the parents, which totally incensed Amy and me. Because one thing we were used to was our parents always wanting us at the dinner table with whoever else happened to be there."

PEG PALMER WEARS

*"I think the press made a grave mistake in calling Arnold,
Jack, and myself 'The Big Three.' I think The Big Three were
Winnie Palmer, Barbara Nicklaus and Vivienne Player."*

Gary Player

Part Three

Arnie versus Jack

Golf's greatest rivalry ever.

Rivalries are the lifeblood of sport. They're at the heart of what

competition is all about. But most athletic lives are short, and individual rivalries tend to fade. Muhammad Ali and Joe Frazier waged wars that remain the pyramids of boxing, but their encounters came and went in four years. Affirmed and Alydar captured the imagination of America, but their battle for horse-racing's triple crown lasted only five weeks. In that regard then, Arnold Palmer and Jack Nicklaus are unique. Never before in the history of sports have two truly great superstars battled each other for as long and as hard as "Arnie and Jack." And more than three decades after their rivalry began, it's still intense.

Jack Nicklaus was born in Ohio on January 21, 1940. His father believed that sports helped mold young men, and Jack had the natural ability to put that belief into practice. In eighth grade, at age 13, he stood five feet ten and weighed 165 pounds; ran a 100-yard dash in 11 seconds flat; played catcher in baseball; and was the starting quarterback, punter and placekicker on his junior high school football team. As a high school basketball player, he started for three years and, in his senior season, averaged 18 points a game on a team that went to the fourth round of the state championship tournament. That same year, he made 26 free throws in a row, and was named "all-league" and "honorable mention all-state."

But Nicklaus's premier sport was golf. Playing at the Scioto Country Club where his father was a

Facing page: The present and future Kings of golf,
Palmer and Nicklaus, 1960 U.S. Open.

member, he shot a 74 at age 12 and 69 one year later. At age 13, he won the Ohio State Junior Championship for boys 15 and under. At 16, he entered the qualifying rounds for the U.S. Open, and incredibly, earned the second alternate spot. As a 19-year-old college sophomore, he was the youngest winner of the USGA Amateur Championship since 1910. And in 1960, still playing as an amateur, he finished second in the U.S. Open with a 282 that remains the lowest score posted by an amateur in U.S. Open history. Then, a year later, he won the USGA Amateur Championship again.

Jack Nicklaus was the stuff of which legends are made, save for one failing that wasn't his fault. Good looks are an unearned privilege. Arnold had them; and Jack didn't. Nicklaus was fat. His height had topped out at five feet ten, and his weight had ballooned to 210 pounds. His girlfriend, whom he later married, called him "Fat Boy" on occasion. To his fraternity brothers at Ohio State, he was "Blob-O." His thighs were thick, his rear end was enormous, and the white cloth on the inside of his pants pockets showed when he bent over to putt. He wasn't warm or charismatic; just an awesomely talented young man with a moon-shaped face, butch haircut, and high squeaky voice, who felt from the moment he arrived on the pro

"The competition has been there from the very beginning; and in my mind, it will go on for as long as we live. We don't socialize; we don't spend a lot of time together. But Jack and I have a deep-seated respect for one another. And if you stop and reflect upon how long we've been at it, I think we've gotten along pretty well over the years. I consider us friends."

ARNOLD PALMER

scene that he was the best golfer in the world and that it was just a matter of time until he proved it.

"I saw Arnold for the first time in 1954, when I was 14 years old," Nicklaus remembers. "I was entered in the Ohio State Amateur Championship at the Sylvania Country Club in Toledo. It was late one afternoon, and the only other person on the course was a fellow hitting 9-irons in the rain. And he was drilling them; I was impressed. I remember asking myself, 'Who is that guy? Boy, is he strong.' And then I learned it was Arnold Palmer, the defending champion. He won the tournament again that year, and the rest is history."

Palmer for his part recalls that he and Nicklaus met formally on a golf course for the first time in 1956. The occasion was an exhibition in Athens, Ohio, to celebrate "Dow Finsterwald Day." Jack was 16, and Arnold was 26. "We had a driving contest," Palmer remembers, "and I beat him by a bit. After that, I kept an eye on him and was aware of what he was doing in golf. You never know how someone's game will develop, but with Jack I figured it was just a matter of time."

Nicklaus turned pro in 1962, but the public eye was elsewhere. Its attention was focused on the renewed possibility that Palmer, who was playing the best golf of his career, would win all four "majors" in the same year to complete golf's mythical "grand slam." He'd already won the Masters in April. And the U.S. Open was about to be held 35 miles from Latrobe at the Oakmont Country Club; a course Palmer had played perhaps a hundred times.

Palmer's fans "knew" he would win the Open. As Dan Jenkins later wrote, "He might have to slash his way through an evergreen along the way, or bounce one off a caddie's jawbone. But one way or another, he would summon a charge and it would be magic time again." Palmer, though, wasn't so sure. Despite having considerable confidence, he understood that golf courses don't play favorites. And for the first time in his pro career, there was a young star emerging behind him. Jack Nicklaus had yet to win on the tour, but he'd been in the money in every tournament he'd entered. And in less than six months, he'd already broken the full-season rookie earnings record. "Everybody says there's only one favorite, and that's me," Palmer observed on the eve of the Open. "But you'd better watch the fat boy."

In the end, 72,000 fans came to Oakmont; 25,000 more than the previous U.S. Open record. Palmer and Nicklaus were paired together for the first two rounds. And as Jerry Izenberg recalls, "Anybody with an IQ of over 40 could see that

something special was building. It wasn't just the size of the crowd or the intensity of the competition. It was the way everything was coming together and everyone interacted."

Palmer was clearly the hometown hero, and thousands of steelworkers from the Pittsburgh area turned out to voice their support. "I thought I was at a wrestling match," Tom Fitzgerald of the *Boston Globe* wrote. Arnie's Army stomped on the ground in unison while Nicklaus was trying to putt. Its members carried signs with messages like "Nicklaus is a pig," and shouted, "Miss it, fat-gut." Meanwhile, Palmer began with rounds of 71 and 68 for a three-stroke lead at the halfway point, and carded a 73 and 71 on "Open Saturday."

To put Palmer's 283 total in perspective, in three previous U.S. Opens at Oakmont, only Ben Hogan and Sam Snead had been able to break 290. But Nicklaus outdid Palmer on the final day of regulation play, closing with a 72 and 69 to tie for first place. That set up an 18-hole playoff on Sunday, and Jack started off hot. After eight holes, he enjoyed a four-stroke advantage. Then Palmer "charged." A birdie on nine . . . Birdie on 11 . . . Birdie on 12 . . . And the lead was down to one.

"After the 12th hole," Nicklaus remembers, "I figured, 'Uh oh; here he comes.' And I said to myself, 'Most people get flustered and start

The loss at the 1962 U.S. Open would prove to be one of the most
painful memories in Palmer's career.

bogeying when he does this. Don't be an idiot; play your own game.' I tried not to think of it as a comeback, but to think that we'd played 12 holes and I was up one."

Then Palmer bogeyed 13, and Jack's lead was two again. It stayed that way until the final hole, where Nicklaus recalls, "I got a little bit scared. I'd played with Jack Burke in practice on Tuesday, and he'd put his drive out of bounds on 18. He'd taken an eight for the hole, and I figured going out of bounds like that could lose it for me. I aimed at the center of the fairway, and hooked about 18 inches into the rough. But that didn't bother me too much. It was better than being out of bounds."

Nicklaus was on the 18th green in three, 12 feet to the left of the cup. Then Palmer pitched his third shot toward the hole, and Jack remembers, "I saw the ball go flying into the air and thought it was going in. I thought, 'Oh, my God; I guess I have to expect it to go in.' But it didn't; it rolled about 10 feet past the hole. After that, my putt went about two feet past the cup. I still wasn't sure of winning. If he makes his putt and I miss mine, we go 19. And a two-footer to win a national championship isn't easy. But he missed his putt, and I finally knew, 'Well, it's over.'"

At age 22, Jack Nicklaus had fashioned a playoff-round 71 to win the U.S. Open by three strokes. In 90 holes of pressure golf, he had three-putted only once. Palmer had played magnificent golf. But in many respects that made his defeat even more disheartening, because he now knew that, even if he played his best, Nicklaus might beat him. Nicklaus could outdrive him; Nicklaus could putt with him; and Jack Nicklaus just might be the better golfer. "I'll tell you something," Palmer said when the 1962 Open was over. "Now that the big guy is out of the cage, everybody better run for cover."

But if anyone thought the King was about to relinquish his throne, they were wrong. The next month, Palmer won his second "major" of the year with an awesome showing in the British Open. His four-round total of 276 was 12 under par, six strokes ahead of the field, and two strokes better than the previous British Open record. "I've never, I mean never, played better golf," Palmer said when the tournament was over. And the *London Observer* was moved to comment, "The American Palmer has been spoken of as the greatest golfer of all time. However exaggerated such a view may sound, Palmer is showing the kind of overwhelming form that makes it possible he may earn that designation before his career comes to an end."

The British Open was Palmer's seventh "major" championship – a feat made even more impressive by the fact that he was only 32 years old,

Palmer en route to victory at the 1962 British Open.

two years younger than Ben Hogan had been when he won the first of his nine major titles. That set the stage for the PGA in August, which Palmer entered as a 2 to 1 favorite. For three rounds, he played the course at par, while Gary Player put on a brilliant display of shot-making to take the lead at eight under. Then, on the final day, Arnold approached the first tee, threw his arms in the air, and announced to the gallery, "I'm going out and shoot this son-of-a-gun in 62." A huge roar followed. The Army believed. But the best Palmer could do was a 72, and Player won going away.

The next week, Palmer rebounded once more to win the American Golf Classic. Then he and Sam Snead captured their second Canada Cup. At year's end, the record book showed that Palmer had entered 23 tournaments, won eight, and again broken golf's single-season earnings record. And 1963 began with more of the same. In the past, Palmer had entered the Los Angeles Open seven times, and never finished better than 10th. But this time he played the first three rounds in eight under par, and closed with a 66 for a three-stroke victory in the first tournament of the season. "Here we go again," Mike Souchak grumped. "New year, same story." Then came victories in the Phoenix and Pensacola opens, and it was time again for the Masters.

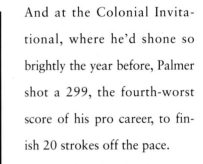

Palmer congratulates Nicklaus on his first Masters championship in 1963.

This year, though, Palmer was never in the chase at Augusta. His four-round total of 291 left him in ninth place, five strokes behind the youngest winner in Masters history – Jack Nicklaus. A week later, Palmer went to San Antonio for the Texas Open and finished ninth for the second time in a row. At the Tournament of Champions in Las Vegas, he lost by five strokes; again to Nicklaus. And at the Colonial Invitational, where he'd shone so brightly the year before, Palmer shot a 299, the fourth-worst score of his pro career, to finish 20 strokes off the pace.

And suddenly, the question was being asked: "What's wrong with Arnold Palmer?" In part, Palmer was the victim of unrealistic expectations spawned by his own talent. Golf is a sport where the champion is always an underdog. Yet, where Arnold was concerned, the public seemed to have forgotten that. Palmer was golf's equivalent of the New York Yankees. Like Sugar Ray Robinson and Joe Louis in their prime, he was supposed to win all the time, and no one is capable of doing that.

But aside from the unreasonable expectations put upon him, Palmer's game appeared to be slipping. "His putting is off," Doug Ford said. "And he's used to putting so phenomenally that a little bad putting comes as a mental jar to him." Bob Rosburg agreed that "Arnold's putting has been affected," and added, "He's lost some of his distance too; he doesn't seem to be catching the ball solid anymore."

But underlying every theory about Palmer's game was the presence of Jack Nicklaus. In the first five months of 1963, Nicklaus had triumphed in three tournaments that Palmer had won the previous year. "Whatever Arnie wants, Jack gets," *Time* magazine said after the 1963 Masters. Writing in *Sports Illustrated*, Alfred Wright declared that Nicklaus had started "a new era before that of Palmer has even begun to ebb." And Doug Sanders spoke for many of his fellow pros when he said, "Baby Beef is doing to Arnie what Palmer did to all the rest of us."

Meanwhile, Palmer spoke of his circumstances in an uncharacteristically introspective manner. "It's not all a bed of roses," he said. "Sometimes I think I would have had a better life if I'd been born 50 years earlier, when the stakes weren't so high and the game was more carefree." But he resisted the notion that Nicklaus had somehow managed to break his will, pointing out, "When I started, Sam Snead was beating me all the time, and I turned the tables. Right now, it's just that I happened to lose three big tournaments that Nicklaus happened to win. He's a wonderful player, but he's still got a long way to go."

And then Palmer did something he'd never done before as a pro. He took a month off from the

tour to relax. "You can't play every tournament and play well," he said, explaining his action. "If you try to make them all, soon you're just another player. I'm not as young as I was, and you age faster if you keep hitting the trail every week."

Had the roller-coaster ride come to an end? Hardly. Returning to the tour in June 1963, Palmer defeated Paul Harney on the first hole of a sudden-death playoff to win the Thunderbird Open. Then he travelled to The Country Club in Brookline, Massachusetts, seeking to regain the U.S. Open crown. For four rounds in Brookline, the golfers were challenged by a difficult course and violent winds. Jack Nicklaus failed to make the cut, which he attributed to "my failure to maintain emotional control." But Palmer persevered and found himself in a three-way tie with Julius Boros and Jackie Cupit at the end of regulation play. Suffering from dysentery the next day, he could do no better than 76 and ceded the Open crown to Boros. For Arnie's Army, the result was a catastrophe. For the second year in a row, he'd lost the U.S. Open in a playoff. But a week later, Palmer was back on track, defeating Tony Lema and Tommy Aaron in a playoff at the Cleveland Open. That meant, over the course of 18 days, he'd won two playoffs, lost one, and earned $54,000, which raised his earnings for the year to a record $85,545. And it wasn't even the Fourth of July.

Then Palmer slipped again. Seeking his third straight British Open title, he carded a 294, which left him in 26th place, 17 strokes behind Bob Charles. And in the PGA, he fell to 40th with a 293, 14 strokes behind a victorious Jack Nicklaus. Once again, the naysayers were out. And once again, Palmer responded. At the Western Open, he took first place, defeating Nicklaus and Boros in a playoff. Then he finished second at the American Golf Classic and first at the Whitemarsh Open, capping a run of eight tournaments during which he placed first four times and second twice.

Meanwhile, as the battle between "Arnie and Jack" raged, the public's hostility toward Nicklaus was mushrooming beyond all reasonable bounds. Americans demand villains for their heroes to slay, and Jack was a storybook rival for Palmer. Arnold was perceived as having succeeded at golf the hard way. Although being the son of a club pro was hardly a disadvantage, he'd been a fighter all his life. Nicklaus, by contrast, was seen as having been given the world on a silver platter. He'd been born into a wealthy family that belonged to one of Ohio's most exclusive country clubs. Growing up, he'd been tutored by the leading golf instructors of his day, and his father had financed his amateur

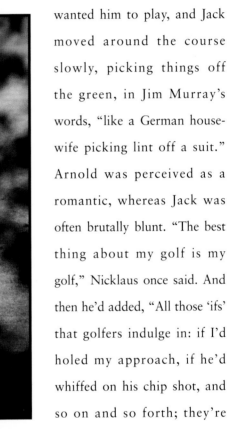

Palmer at the 1963 Thunderbird Classic.

travels. After Arnold and Winnie eloped, they'd lived in a trailer. When Nicklaus and his fiancée, Barbara Bash, got married, his parents gave them the down payment for a house.

Arnold was "a regular guy," whereas Nicklaus was "a whale with a computer heart." Arnold had a natural rapport with people, while Jack held them at arm's length. Arnold played golf the way his fans wanted him to play, and Jack moved around the course slowly, picking things off the green, in Jim Murray's words, "like a German housewife picking lint off a suit." Arnold was perceived as a romantic, whereas Jack was often brutally blunt. "The best thing about my golf is my golf," Nicklaus once said. And then he'd added, "All those 'ifs' that golfers indulge in: if I'd holed my approach, if he'd whiffed on his chip shot, and so on and so forth; they're absolutely ridiculous. In golf, what didn't take place didn't take place, and that's the end of it."

But Nicklaus's most grievous sin was that he was beating "Arnie." Invariably, when a beloved champion is on the ropes, the public roots against his challenger. The upstart is viewed as too cocky or spoiled; someone who hasn't paid his dues or proven himself worthy of the throne. And in Nicklaus's case, not only was he 22 years old when he beat Palmer at Oakmont, he did and said the sort of things that 22-year-olds say and do. "Do you know how long anybody remembers who finished second: about 30 minutes," Jack had asked rhetorically and answered after winning his first U.S. Open title.

Then in late 1963, another careless remark brought trouble. One year earlier, the World Series of Golf had been inaugurated at the Firestone Country Club in Akron. The participants – Nicklaus, Palmer and Gary Player – had been invited by virtue of having won 1962's four "major" titles. First-place money for the 36-hole event was $50,000; more than any tournament prize ever. And Nicklaus had won. Now the World Series of Golf was being contested again. Nicklaus had been invited because he'd won the Masters and PGA. Julius Boros and Bob Charles were on hand as the U.S. and British Open champions. And to fill out the field, the event organizers invited Palmer after a special "qualifying playoff." Then, the day before the Series began, Arnold and Jack met with reporters, and Nicklaus chided, "If this is a contest for champions only, then Arnold doesn't belong here. Arnie's strictly an also-ran in the major events. The World Series should have winners, not also-rans. Isn't that right, Arnie?"

> *"Arnold and I have had a rivalry in everything we've done. We're competitive in golf; we're competitive in business; we're competitive in endorsing products. And in most respects, it's been a very healthy rivalry. Both of us have benefited from the competition. But I've said it before, and I'll say it again. I don't like to be beat by Arnold, and I'm sure he feels the same way about me. There's no one in the world I'd rather beat than Arnold."*
>
> JACK NICKLAUS

The remark was made in jest, but not everyone took it that way. The next day, the *Akron Beacon Journal* ran a headline that read: "Jack Labels Arnie an 'Also-Ran.'" United Press International wired a comparable story across the country. And just in case there wasn't enough salt in the wound, Nicklaus proceeded to win the World Series for the second year in a row. Now Arnie's Army was angrier than ever and vented its wrath with a cruelty rarely seen in sports. Gary Player remembers, "They'd cheer when Jack got a bogey, and stand by bunkers with signs saying, 'Hit it here, Ohio Fats.' They cursed and spat and did everything possible to torment a very decent young man. At times it must have seemed to Jack as though the whole world was against him. I don't know how he stood up to it. A lesser person surely would have crumbled."

But Nicklaus didn't crumble, although he was very hurt by it all. His biographer, Herbert Warren Wind, recalls, "Jack is rather sensitive, and it was terribly hard for him to have everyone rooting against him. He was very frank with me about how it bothered him that the galleries didn't take to him at all." And Nicklaus himself would say later, "Everyone likes to think of himself as a basically appealing fellow. I know I do. Being as honest

"It was a heated rivalry, full of emotion, with glorious highs and bitter disappointments for both men. And they've gone for 30 years without any lapse in class or in any way publicly disparaging each other. They're true sportsmen; both of them. They always have been and always will be."

BOB COSTAS

as I can, I think of myself as fundamentally companionable; a shade more sensitive than I appear to be, a bit too direct on occasion, a bit too stubborn on others; but a good deal less cold and grim and cocksure than some people read me as being. I'm aware that I'm not the matinee-idol type. Rooms don't light up when I enter. And I'd be less than candid if I didn't say that there have been moments when I wished I'd come up when golf had a less glamorous idol."

But like it or not, Palmer was golf's idol. And when 1963 came to an end, Arnold was still "number one." He hadn't won a "major" during the year, but he'd prevailed in seven official tournaments out of 20 entered. And once again, he was in first place on the official tour earnings list with $128,230 in prize money: $28,000 ahead of the second-place Nicklaus.

That set the stage for 1964, which began on a down note for Palmer. At times he played well, with top-three finishes at the Lucky International and the Los Angeles and Pensacola Opens. But he failed to win any of the first 10 tournaments he entered, and missed the cut at the Bing Crosby Pro-Am – the first time that had happened to him in 62 tour events dating back to January 1961. The Crosby was also notable anecdotally because, after Palmer had been eliminated,

The Big Three: Palmer, Player and Nicklaus, seen here at the 1962 World Series of Golf.

he went to the press room and patiently explained the sextuplet-bogey on the 17th hole that had eliminated him from play. "What other golfer who scored a nine on one hole would meet with the press and be that gracious?" one onlooker wondered aloud. To which a reporter responded, "What other golfer who scored a nine on one hole would be invited?"

Nonetheless, the bottom line was, when Palmer arrived at the Masters in Augusta, Jack Nicklaus was the pre-tournament favorite. And for the first time in eight years, Arnold was there without a tour victory to his credit. Still, as Alfred Wright later wrote, "Something special goes on between Palmer and the Masters." And at a time when Arnold needed it most, he made the 1964 Masters his own to win the ceremonial green jacket for an unprecedented fourth time.

Palmer began his historic triumph with rounds of 69 and 68, to lead by four strokes after 36 holes. A third-round 69 moved him five shots ahead of the field. And his four-round total of 276, the second lowest in Masters history, left the competition six strokes behind. "There's no way I can explain how important that tournament was to me," Palmer said later. But he tried at the time, telling the assembled media, "This was the most

"*I played with Arnold in the last round of the 1964 Masters. It was Easter Sunday,
a magnificent day. And it was the first time I'd played well in one of the majors. He had a five-
or six-shot lead going into the last round, so we were together in the final pairing. And I remember,
we were playing the 15th hole. Arnold still had that five- or six-shot lead. Nicklaus had finished,
and I was trying to catch him for second. And Arnold had a shot that was borderline as to whether
or not he should try to knock it across the water. Anyone else with that lead would have played
it safe, so of course Arnold went for it. He hit a monster shot, and he lost sight of the ball as it
passed through the glare of the sun off the lake. He couldn't see where it landed, so he asked me,
'Did it get over?' And I told him, 'Hell, Arnold; your divot got over.'*"

DAVE MARR

Palmer misses an eagle putt during the 1964 Masters.
Nonetheless, he went on to capture his fourth and final Masters title.

exciting single tournament of my life. I played here the way I'd like to play in every tournament. You know, I started this year unhappy about some of the things I'd done last year. And one thing I was very definite about in my mind was, if I did nothing else, I'd try my best to win at least one major championship this year. I can't say I was aiming particularly at the Masters, although that's the one I wanted first." And then Palmer added what everyone knew: "It's harder to stay on a pedestal than to get there."

The following week, Nicklaus knocked Palmer off his pedestal at least temporarily by winning the Tournament of Champions. Two weeks later, Palmer returned the favor, capturing the Oklahoma City Open. Then, in late May, Arnold teamed with Dwight Eisenhower in the former president's only public golf performance on record – a benefit for the Heart Association of Southeastern Pennsylvania. And after that, he began a remarkable string of seven tournaments in a row in which he finished second five times and third twice. That run would have exhilarated almost any other golfer, but Palmer wasn't satisfied with it. Finishing second was less than a win. And perhaps more important, he needed wins because he and Nicklaus were locked in a duel to determine who would be golf's leading money-winner for 1964; a title that was particularly significant because, until 1970, golfers

These commemorative gold coins were awarded to Palmer for his Masters victories in 1958, 1960, 1962 and 1964.

were officially ranked by tour earnings.

Thus, it came to pass that what might have been the most significant battle ever waged between Arnold Palmer and Jack Nicklaus occurred, not at the Masters or U.S. Open, but in a small Louisiana town at a tournament known as the Cajun Classic. Winter was approaching. Palmer was ranked first on the official earnings list with $111,703 in prize money; Nicklaus was $319 behind; and there was one tour event left in the year.

The prize money for the Cajun Classic started at a meager $3,300 for first place and dropped precipitously from there. But "Arnie and Jack" were at the Oakbourne Country Club in Lafayette, Louisiana, where neither man had dreamed he'd be entered earlier in the year. "It's a matter of personal pride," Nicklaus said, explaining why he and Palmer were there. "Winning the official earnings title is a real measure of accomplishment; the next best thing to a major championship."

It's possible that sports has never witnessed a more important event played in less likely surroundings. Sportswriter Gwilym Brown later wrote, "It all seemed like a comical mistake, as if the Army-Navy game had been scheduled in a high school gym." The first day of the tournament was washed out by a violent thunderstorm. Then the weather turned cold, which Brown observed, "would have been fine for the Dartmouth Winter

Carnival or pheasant hunting in Latrobe, but not for golf." Because of the rainout, the final 36 holes were played on Sunday. Nicklaus teed off at 8:12 a.m. with 18 people in the gallery watching. He was wearing three sweaters and a rainsuit; and by the time he reached the third hole, the damp towel hanging from his golf bag was frozen. Meanwhile, for one of the few times in his career, Palmer was wearing a hat on the course, not to mention layers of sweaters.

Neither man won. That honor went to Miller Barber. Palmer finished fourth, which was worth $1,500. And in the end, the battle for supremacy between Arnold and Jack came down to a 16-foot putt on the final hole by Gay Brewer. If Brewer made the putt, he'd finish in second place and Nicklaus in third; not good enough for Jack to overcome Palmer's original

Palmer battles the elements at the 1964 Cajun Classic.

lead of $319 plus the $1,500 Arnold had just won. But if Brewer missed, Nicklaus would be tied for second, which would earn him $1,900. "What's it worth to you if I miss it?" Brewer asked moments before he putted. In response, Jack reached into his pocket, took out a well-filled money clip, and thrust it forward. "It was the first putt I couldn't bring myself to watch since the six-footer Palmer missed that would have beaten me

in the 1962 Open," Nicklaus said later. Meanwhile, Brewer lined up his putt . . . stroked it . . . and came up short.

Golf had a new king. After 41 tournaments, Jack Nicklaus was the year's leading money-winner by a margin of $81. And two months later, on his 25th birthday, Nicklaus spoke frankly of his goals for the future:

"My ambition is to be the greatest golfer who ever lived, just as it's Arnold's ambition and everyone else's who plays the game seriously. But we have different ways of going at it. Arnold wants to win the Grand Slam, because he'd like to do something that no one has ever done before. I don't know yet what I'll have to do to become the greatest. I remind myself that I'm only 25, whereas Arnold didn't reach his peak until he was 29 and Hogan until he was 36. Right now, I think you'd have to say that Hogan was the best ever. That's my goal, but I don't know how to get there. Maybe I could win the Grand Slam, but what would I do after that if I was still young. Win two Grand Slams?"

Meanwhile, as Nicklaus's star was rising, Palmer's appeared to be in descent. "The golf ball doesn't appreciate that you're a hotshot player, nor does the course," he acknowledged later. "It's a clean sheet every time you play, and you have to impress them with your talent all over again. Nobody ever hit a ball with his reputation."

And despite his reputation, for the first time in his career, Palmer seemed to be genuinely foundering. In 1965, for the second year in a row, he arrived at the Masters without a victory. This time though, despite being tied for first at the halfway point, he was unable to prevail. Instead, Nicklaus fired closing rounds of 64 and 69 for a 271 total that shattered Ben Hogan's Masters record by three shots and consigned Palmer to second place, a distant nine strokes back. Then, at the U.S. Open, Palmer scored opening rounds of 76 and 76, failed to record a birdie, and missed the cut in golf's most prestigious tournament for the first time in eight years. That was followed by a 16th-place finish at the British Open. And the year's fourth "major" brought more of the same.

The PGA was the only Grand Slam event that Palmer had never won, and in 1965 it was held at his home course, the Laurel Valley Golf Club in Ligonier, Pennsylvania. But Palmer was never in the running. He failed to break par for any round and finished in 33rd place, 14 strokes behind Dave Marr. Now, unlike 1963, "Arnie's slump" was for real. By the end of the year, he'd won only one tournament in the preceeding 19 months. After five

> *"The fact that Arnold never won the PGA is irrelevant. Nobody would have held it against Sam Snead if he hadn't won the PGA. The U.S. Open [which Snead never won] is the big one; and after that, the Masters. Arnold never won the PGA? So what! That's the PGA's loss."*
>
> BOB DRUM

consecutive years of ranking first or second on the official tour earnings list, he'd fallen to 10th place, $83,000 behind Nicklaus.

"It was not a good year," Palmer conceded as 1965 came to an end. But more compelling than his admission of the obvious was the need to understand the reasons why. Some observers pointed to Arnold's burgeoning business interests as a source of distraction that had hampered his golf. Others noted that he seemed fatigued, was suffering from bursitis in his shoulder, and at age 36 needed more rest. Then there was the matter of his having given up smoking. Palmer had smoked two packs a day for years, and rarely played more than a hole without lighting up a cigarette. That was good for Liggett & Myers, the tobacco company to which he licensed his image for use in a major advertising campaign. But in 1964, the Surgeon General of the United States had issued a report linking cigarette smoking to various illnesses including heart disease and lung cancer. Palmer had begun getting letters from doctors and teachers, telling him that he was setting a bad example for the youth of America. And in addition, he suffered periodically from inflamed ears and sinus problems. Thus, when his contract with L&M expired, rather than renew for another year, Arnold had decided to "go cold turkey."

*"Not winning the PGA Championship hurt my pride a little, but it hasn't really affected my life.
I wanted to win it; I want to win every tournament I enter. But the press made more
out of it than was really the case. It doesn't haunt me."*

ARNOLD PALMER

When Palmer gave up smoking, he gained 15 pounds and began to drink a little more at parties. But initially at least, his golf didn't seem to be affected. Asked how the decision had changed his life, he said simply, "I find I can sign autographs a lot faster without a cigarette in my hand." But by late 1964, his resolve had begun to waver. And by 1965, he was smoking regularly off the course although not on it. He didn't want the public to know he'd failed, and he was conscious of his status as a role model for children. But that meant, at crucial points in a tournament when his need for a cigarette was greatest, he couldn't have one. "I urged Arnie strongly to give up smoking," Dwight Eisenhower said in August 1965. "He took my advice; and by golly, he hasn't been the same since."

But at the heart of everything, regardless of its cause, was the fact that Palmer had lost his putting touch. Putting is different from the rest of golf. There's no one way to be a good putter. But virtually everyone in golf acknowledges that the ability to hole putts from eight feet and less is what separates superstars from also-rans.

When Palmer was at the peak of his game, he'd been the best long putter in the history of golf. "I don't think I'm putting any better now than I did when I was a kid," he'd said in 1960. "When you're a kid, you're not scared of anything. You go for

> *"The mechanical side of putting is hardly worth mentioning. You can hold the putter any way you like. You can use any kind of stance you want. Some people are wrist putters; others are arm putters. It's up to the individual. There's only one mechanical secret to putting, and this is holding still. Your body has to be totally motionless while you stroke the ball."*
>
> ARNOLD PALMER

everything and slide by lots of the time, but they go in too." As the years passed, all of golf had become familiar with the Palmer creed: "There are no rules for putting except for the basic truth: if it works, it's right. It's an instinctive function . . . I guess I putt past the pin more than most everybody. I always like to give it a chance . . . The correct number of putts that should be taken by a good golfer is one per green . . . The way to hole a putt is not to try. Just do it." But putting for a living is very hard on a person's insides. Golfers might not bleed like prizefighters, but their ulcer rate is high. And in 1965, to quote Winnie Palmer, "Arnie suddenly discovered that every putt does not have to go in the hole. The big difference between Jack and Arnie right now is confidence," she said after the 1965 Masters. "Last night, Arnie was certain he was the worst putter who ever stepped onto a golf course. It doesn't occur to Jack that he can miss a putt. It's when you get older that you realize you can miss them."

Later, Palmer would reflect on his difficulties of 1965 and explain, "I'd get close, and my hands would begin to shake. I just didn't think I could win; and I really didn't know if I was ever going to win again." But at the time, there was little for him to say except, "I don't know what's wrong with my game. I can't explain it. I'm just missing the three- and

"If I ever had to stake the family jewels on a single eight-foot putt, I'd want Palmer to putt it for me. He exerts so much physical and mental force, it's almost as though he commands the ball to obey him."

BYRON NELSON

"*Jack wouldn't want me to tell you this, but we were in a tournament years ago,*
playing together, and Arnold was on the adjacent fairway. Jack was shooting about a 64, leading
the tournament; Arnold a 74, and out of it. But all the people were over there, crashing
through the rough and raising hell. Jack was on the green. He stopped to look, and he said,
'One of these days, those so-and-so's will be over here.' It bothered him all right."

GARDNER DICKINSON

four-footers and not making anything. And when that happens, the good rounds become mediocre, and the bad ones go down real low." And as for the future, Palmer said simply, "Facing up to a challenge is what sport is all about. I've been on top for nine years now, and it would be interesting to see what would happen to some other people in the same circumstances. It's being on top that affects your game."

And then, to the delight of his fans and the astonishment of just about everyone else in golfdom, Palmer began 1966 with the best start any pro had enjoyed on the tour since the 1940s. In the year's first tournament, the Los Angeles Open, he birdied seven holes in a row en route to a third-round 62 and a three-stroke victory over Miller Barber and Paul Harney. Then, in successive weeks, he finished second, third, and second in the Bing Crosby Pro-Am, Lucky International, and Bob Hope Desert Classic. Now Arnie was sinking 30-foot putts and smoking cigarettes openly again. "My only objective this year is winning golf tournaments," he told reporters. "That's what interests me. I keep on, not for the prize money or for how it helps me in my other interests, but because I think I can win. If you're not competing one way or another, you're dead." In other words, Arnie was Arnie again.

Next up was the Phoenix Open, a tournament Palmer had won on three of the previous four occasions he'd entered. But in Phoenix, Arnold's run ended. He played mediocre golf, and finished in 34th place. Two weeks later, he was 36th at the Florida Citrus Open. And despite respectable showings at the Doral and Greensboro Opens, he arrived at the Masters with a question mark over his head again. Palmer played well at Augusta. After 62 holes, he was tied for the lead, and a fifth Masters title seemed possible. But then he faltered and faded to fourth, two strokes behind Tommy Jacobs, Gay Brewer, and Nicklaus. That led to an 18-hole playoff on Monday, and all Arnold could do was watch.

Two years earlier, Palmer had said, "Of greatest importance to me is becoming the first Masters champion to successfully defend at Augusta. This has moved to the front of my list, not only because nobody has accomplished it, but because I failed twice when I should have won." However, in April 1966, it was Nicklaus, with a two-stroke playoff victory, who became the first man in history to successfully defend the Masters crown. The victory was Jack's third in four years at Augusta. And although Palmer rebounded the following week to win the Tournament of Champions, the "major" tournaments that defined his career were now losses more often than wins. There was a need to prove himself anew if he were to be considered the best golfer in the world again. And that opportunity came dramatically in June at the Olympic Country Club in San Francisco – the site of the 66th U.S. Open.

The first round of the Open belonged to Al Mengert, a little-known pro who shot a 67. But the next day, Palmer caught fire with a 66 to tie Billy Casper for the lead at 137. The final two rounds were played on Saturday and Sunday, the tradition of "Open Saturday" having been abandoned in 1965. In round three, Palmer carded a 70 to move three strokes ahead of the field. And on Sunday, he began with a spectacular 32 on the front nine, opening up a seven-stroke lead. The Open was won; or so it seemed. Casper, who was paired with Palmer, essentially conceded as much on the 10th fairway when he told Arnold, "I'm going to have to really go just to get second." And Palmer assured him, "Don't worry, Bill; you'll finish second." But that was when something changed. Rather than concentrate on winning, Palmer began to focus instead on breaking Ben Hogan's 1948 Open record of 276. All he needed was a 36 on the back nine for a total of 275. And the result was disaster.

"Some people don't want to know comparative scores," Palmer once told a reporter. "But I'm not that isolated. I'll take a glance at the

> *"Did I learn anything from San Francisco? Well, just put me in the Open with a seven-stroke lead and nine holes to play again, and I promise I won't let that opportunity slip by a second time."*
>
> ARNOLD PALMER

scoreboard or cock my ear to catch what Finsterwald or Snead or Hogan is doing. I like to know what's going on with the other players." However, on the back nine at Olympic, Arnold didn't have to look far to learn what was happening. Billy Casper was right beside him.

• No.10: Palmer scored a bogey-5, and his lead was cut to six.

• No.11: Palmer and Casper both scored pars.

• No.12: Both men scored birdies. Palmer's lead was still six with six holes left to play. "The worst break of all could have been that birdie," he said later. "It convinced me I could break the record."

• No.13: Palmer missed the green with his tee shot, and settled for a bogey-4. His lead was now five.

• No.14: Both men made their par. Palmer was still five up, and only four holes remained.

• No.15: Another par-3. "I was trying to play the perfect shot," Palmer acknowledged later. "I really enjoy shooting at the pin. I grew up thinking that's what you're supposed to do." So Arnold attempted a "perfect shot," watched his ball roll into a bunker, and ended up with a bogey. Meanwhile, Casper went for the center of the green, and holed a 20-foot birdie putt. The lead was three with three holes left. "And for the first time," Palmer remembers, "it dawned on me that Billy had a chance."

• No.16: The same philosophy that had spurred

Palmer to his greatest triumphs now threatened defeat. "I knew I could just bump the ball down the fairway a couple of times, knock it on the green, take a par, and the game was over," he said later. "That's what a lot of smart golfers might have done. Casper, in fact, was just playing it safe. That's what really got me. Here's a guy trying to catch me, and he was the one playing safe. I said to myself, 'There's no way that man can beat me.' And I wasn't going to let it be said, 'There goes Palmer, using a one-iron to be safe with a three-stroke lead.' I'd rather lose."

Palmer's first shot on the par-5 16th hole hit a tree and bounced into deep rough. His second, a 3-iron, travelled less than a hundred yards. The best he could do was his second bogey in a row. And Casper, who was "playing it safe," scored his second consecutive birdie. Palmer had now lost four strokes on two holes, and his lead was one.

• No.17: Casper scored his third birdie in a row, and the U.S. Open was tied.

Palmer drove poorly on the 72nd hole and needed a superb second shot to match Casper's par. Both men finished at 278. "I still can't believe it happened," Palmer said later. "All I could think was, 'I've just lost a seven-shot lead in the U.S. Open, and now I've got to tell the press exactly how I did it.'" But true to his nature, Arnold went to the press tent, and answered questions for what must have seemed to him like an eternity. Then came the playoff, which Casper won by four strokes. And as far as Arnie's Army was concerned, the flags on the greens should have been lowered to half-staff. "It's a funny thing about that Open," Arnold would say long after it was over. "I think what beat me in the playoff was the memory of the day before. And people felt so sorry for me afterward. They cared so damn much." And Palmer cared too – a lot. A quarter-century later, when the U.S. Open returned to Olympic, Rick Reilly went to interview Palmer for a 1966 Open retrospective. "Arnold didn't want to do it," Reilly recalls. "In the end, he did. And he was polite the whole time; I don't mean to suggest otherwise. But even though it was 25 years later, Olympic was obviously still a very painful memory for him."

The loss at Olympic was particularly devastating to Palmer because it came at a crucial time in his career. He was still playing excellent golf, and would do so for many years. He was still the most popular golfer in the world, and that would never change. But his "charges" were growing fewer in number, with weeks and sometimes months in between. He wasn't winning "majors" anymore. And faced with the opportunity to return to the top of the competitive heap, he had come in second. By his own demanding standard, he had failed. Now it was beyond dispute that Jack Nicklaus was the best golfer in the world. "Nicklaus measures his achievements against history," Dave Kindred later wrote. "For Nicklaus, Bobby Jones is par." And Jones, for his part, said simply, "Jack is playing an entirely different game – a game I'm not even familiar with."

As the years passed, Nicklaus's memories of the 1960s would continue to be tinged with pain. Long after he had won more "majors" than anyone else in the history of golf, he would look back on the 1960 U.S. Open at Cherry Hills and wonder, "what would have happened if I or somebody else didn't shoot bad on the back nine the final round. Arnold wouldn't have won. He might never have gained the popularity and all. You wonder if things might have been different." And even today, having long been accepted by the public as the greatest golfer ever, Jack thinks of the past and says, "Arnold played a role in my growing up. It wasn't easy. In fact, it was very tough for me to compete against Arnold and his gallery. But in retrospect, it was a learning experience, probably one of the best experiences I've ever had. I became a better person and a better

"I think a lot of the change in Jack's image – losing weight, letting his hair grow longer, dressing more stylishly – was done with Arnold in mind. It wasn't so much an attempt to emulate Arnold as an effort to become more accepted by the public. And when the galleries finally began to appreciate Jack, the world became a much easier, brighter place for him."

HERBERT WARREN WIND

player as a result, although I wasn't always aware of that as I was going through it."

And Palmer too bears scars. "My brother never said anything to me in private about Jack that was different from what he said in public," Jerry Palmer remembers. "He admired Jack. He respected the way Jack played golf. And it made him mad when Jack beat him, because Arnie has always been a very competitive, very proud guy." But Palmer's hurt went deeper than the loss of a two-man sports competition. "It was hard for Arnold when Jack came along," Jerry Izenberg recalls. "One day, he was King of the World. And then, probably as early as the U.S. Open at Oakmont, he had to sense that it was just a matter of time before Jack became number one. Nobody likes having their mantle stolen. That throne belonged to Palmer; and the truth is, without Jack, who knows how long Arnold would have reigned? But Palmer handled it with remarkable grace. He kept on trying; he never complained. He was an exemplary sportsman in every sense of the word. And in the end, really, he had no choice; because Nicklaus winning was as inevitable as night. I suppose what happened was, fate whispered in Jack's ear, 'I'll make you the greatest golfer of all time.' And then it told Arnold, 'Don't worry; the people will always love you more.'"

*"No one ever played golf in a finer spirit or set a finer pattern of behavior
in adversity or success than Arnold Palmer."*

P.J. WARD-THOMAS

It's harder to stay on a pedestal than to get there.

"People who talk about choking under pressure have no idea how many things can go wrong on a golf course besides nerves and fear."
ARNOLD PALMER

"When a golfer changes his putter, things might go well for about a week because having something new gives him confidence. But then the new putter gets to know him, and things turn sour again. It's the Indian, not the arrow."

"We've all watched that scene at the Masters or U.S. Open, where the leader comes down the fairway to the final green with the crowd cheering. And with Arnold Palmer, that scene was as exhilarating and thrilling as anything in sports."
DICK SCHAAP

Palmer rams home a putt to win the Masters for an unprecedented fourth time.

Palmer's participant badge from the 1964 Masters.

"The most important thing I can tell you about Arnold and myself is, regardless of anything that might have divided us over the years, both of us believe with everything that's in us in the traditions of the game, the integrity of the game, the way the game is played, and the code of conduct that people should follow on and around a golf course. Those things are very important to Arnold and myself. Neither of us wants to see them lost. We've stood together on those issues for a long time, and I'm sure we'll continue to stand together on them as long as we're both here to take a stand."

JACK NICKLAUS

Above: Jack Nicklaus helps the 1964 Masters champion into his green jacket.
Facing page: Palmer in trouble during the 1963 U.S. Open playoff against Julius Boros.

QUESTION: *Assemble a field of the greatest golfers ever – Bobby Jones, Ben Hogan, Harry Varden, Arnold Palmer, Jack Nicklaus, Walter Hagen, Gene Sarazen, Byron Nelson, Sam Snead, Gary Player. Give them whatever time they need to get used to using contemporary equipment. And then let them play the four "majors" against each other. The Masters at Augusta; the U.S. Open at Baltusrol; the British Open at St. Andrews; and the PGA at Pebble Beach. How do they fare in each tournament?*

ARNOLD PALMER: *Byron Nelson wins them all. In 1945, Byron Nelson was the greatest golfer of all time. The man won eleven tournaments in a row. Some people say it was the war and lack of competition, but that's bull. In 1945, Byron Nelson was as close to a machine as anyone who ever played golf. I'm sure a lot of people would disagree with me; but you asked the question, and that's my answer.*

"Olympic was the low point for me as far as watching Arnold was concerned. Arnold and I played all three practice rounds together. And after the last one, he told me, 'I think I'll break 280.' I said, 'Arnold, you're crazy. The Open was here 11 years ago, and 287 was the best anyone could do.' So he bet me $10 that he'd break 280. And he did; he shot 278. But I never gave him the money, because I didn't want to remind him of how awful that back nine was for him. Why don't you tell him that story, and we'll see if Arnold asks me for the $10. He can be pretty tight with a dollar."
DAVE MARR

Palmer at the 1966 U.S. Open.

Palmer's tools of the trade during the 1960s.

"After Arnold lost that seven-stroke lead at Olympic, he had to come into the press tent for an interview. And while he was answering questions, a huge mob gathered outside. When the interview was over, I told him, 'You don't want to go through that crowd. There's another route we can take, out the side, past the tennis courts. The mob won't see you.' And Arnold answered, 'No; I deserve whatever they do to me.'"

BOB SOMMERS

"The three losses that hurt Arnold the most were the Masters in 1961, Oakmont in 1962, and the Open in 1966. In '61, Arnold was one hole away from becoming the first man to win the Masters two years in a row. He had it, and he lost it. Oakmont was supposed to be his tournament, and he outplayed Jack everywhere but on the greens where his putter left him. And Olympic, when he all but had the tournament and Ben Hogan's record in his pocket and they slipped away, has been an open wound for years."

DOC GIFFIN

Above and facing page: Palmer in defeat at the 1966 U.S. Open.

"I was in New York for a big dinner some years ago. There'd been some sort of vote to decide who was the greatest golfer ever. I was sitting at the dais with Arnold, Hogan, Nicklaus, and a couple of others. And when they announced that Jack had won, Arnold and Ben sort of dropped their heads. Still, I think it was the right decision. You see, you have to understand the difference in golf between a swinger and a hitter. When a hitter is on, he's hard to beat; but a swinger will beat a hitter over a long period of time. Hogan was a swinger; probably the best shot-maker who ever lived. And Arnold was a hitter. But then Jack came along, and he could do both."

SAM SNEAD

"The world's largest private army" on the march at Augusta, 1966.

The Arnold Palmer signature golf ball.

Part Four

We all Grow Older

Palmer's 1967 L.A. Open
championship money clip.

After his devastating U.S. Open loss at Olympic, Palmer played out

the year with victories at the Australian Open and Houston Champions International. He teamed with Jack Nicklaus to win the Canada Cup and PGA Team Championship, and finished third on the official earnings list with $110,468. By the standards of most professional golfers, it would have been a career season. But from Palmer's point of view, it was anything but. For the second year in a row, he'd failed to win a "major." He'd blown a seven-stroke lead to lose the biggest prize his sport had to offer. And Jack Nicklaus had captured the Masters and British Open to further the notion that he, not Arnold, was the best golfer in the world. Still, looking back on 1966, there were several saving graces for Palmer. He'd played well;

and beyond that, it was fast becoming apparent that he no longer needed to win on the tour for his financial future to be secure.

The seeds of Palmer's financial security had been sown years earlier. Prior to the 1960s, athletes, if they were lucky, opened steak houses. Lucrative appearance fees and endorsement contracts for products other than athletic equipment were rare, and Palmer had been an example of how the system worked. In 1959, he was possibly the most exciting golfer in America. He'd already won his first Masters, and was considered by many to be Ben Hogan's heir apparent. Yet he was bound to Wilson Sporting Goods by a contract that guaranteed him only $6,500 a year. For lending his name to Heinz

Facing page: At the Masters in 1969.

ketchup, he received $500 and all the ketchup he could use. His total income from endorsements, personal appearances, instructional articles and the like was $20,000. And by prevailing standards, that was a lot. Then, in 1959, Palmer shook hands with a young Cleveland attorney named Mark McCormack. Their understanding was that, while McCormack would continue his own legal practice, he would also serve as Arnold's business manager and would work only for Palmer where marketing was concerned. That handshake changed the economics of sports.

Before McCormack, no one had understood the extent to which major sports personalities could be linked to profitable business ventures off the playing field. No one had looked at Joe DiMaggio and said, "This guy can be a spokesman for our bank," or "I'll bet he can sell cars." But McCormack had a theory – that Americans love athletes; and where Palmer in particular was concerned, they trusted "Arnie" and wanted to help him. Thus, McCormack approached various corporations with the suggestion that they license Palmer's name as a way of identifying their products with "the Palmer standard of excellence." "Arnold Palmer is a brand name," McCormack

Arnold Palmer and Mark McCormack, in a partnership based on a handshake, would change the economics of professional sport.

told them. "When you license the Palmer name, you're buying an image of quality, goodness, honesty and sincerity. And a licensing agreement with Arnold will cost you far less than it would cost to build a brand name from scratch."

"If I hadn't had Arnold to work with," McCormack says today, "I don't know what would have happened. Arnold had that magical something." But McCormack did have Palmer, and the results were astonishing. In 1962, three years after the Palmer-McCormack relationship began, Arnold's total tour earnings were $82,456. But his income for the year from sources as diverse as endorsement contracts and a new TV show called "Challenge Golf" totaled a half-million dollars. "And we're just getting started," McCormack said.

There was simply no precedent for the kind of merchandising empire that Mark McCormack was building around Arnold Palmer. By 1966, Palmer was endorsing shaving cream, soft drinks, deodorant, power tools and automobiles. But more important, he was President of Arnold Palmer Enterprises – a six-division company headquartered in Cleveland that, among its many activities, licensed sportswear, produced TV and radio shows, franchised putting courses and driving ranges, and arranged the approximately 20 exhibitions at $5,000 per exhibition that Arnold appeared in annually. Numerous single-purpose companies had also been created for activities that ranged from selling insurance to running motels. The Arnold Palmer Golf Company was headquartered in Tennessee, and distributed golf equipment made by various manufacturers in accord with specifications determined by Palmer. More than 100 Arnold Palmer dry-cleaning centers had been franchised at an average franchise fee of $30,000. ("If I don't do well in my next tournament, it will be because I have dishpan hands," Palmer quipped.) Indeed, Palmer's empire was so far reaching that *Sports Illustrated* observed, "The way he has been expanding, everyone may soon be flying to the moon in an Arnold Palmer rocket and staying in an Arnold Palmer motel overlooking the Arnold Palmer crater." And McCormack was quoted in the *Wall Street Journal* as saying, "Arnold has reached the point where his on-course successes aren't terribly important to his enterprises anymore."

The Palmer brand name and standard of excellence launched in the early 1960s would evolve into a multimillion dollar business.

But Palmer's on-course successes were most definitely still important to Palmer, and 1967 brought more of the frustration that came with being the second-best golfer in the world. But then a window of opportunity appeared. In the year's first 12 tournaments, Arnold played exceptionally well, posting wins at the Los Angeles and Tucson Opens; finishing second three times, third twice, and fourth once. Meanwhile, Nicklaus was going through a mini-slump. And by the time the U.S. Open came to the Baltusrol Golf Club in New Jersey, Jack had won only one tournament, missed the cut at the Masters, and trailed Palmer by $59,892 on the official earnings list. If Arnold could win the Open, in the eyes of many he'd be number one again.

After two rounds at Baltusrol, Arnold and Jack were tied for first place. And to heighten the drama, they were paired together for the third round. But playing together on Saturday, they all but forgot about the rest of the field and focused almost exclusively on each other. That resulted in seven holes of mediocre golf, enabling Billy Casper to take the lead. Then, on the eighth tee, Nicklaus turned to Palmer and suggested, "Let's stop playing each other and play the golf course." Meanwhile, the gallery left no doubt as to who it was rooting for, as typified by its response to play on the 17th hole. A Palmer wedge shot landed six feet from the pin, and Arnie's Army erupted in a sustained ovation that increased in volume as he walked onto the green. Meanwhile, Nicklaus was met by silence, save for a lone voice that cried out, "That's all right, Jack. I'm for you." And then Nicklaus did something that might have been expected of Palmer. He tipped his visor in the direction of his fan, and sank a 12-foot birdie putt.

The final round began with Palmer, Nicklaus, and Casper tied for second, one stroke off Marty Fleckman's lead. Arnold and Jack were paired again. And Palmer did what he had to do. He went out and shot a 69 for a four-round total of 279. Under normal circumstances, that would have been enough to win the U.S. Open. But Nicklaus was on a roll, and birdied 10 of the tournament's last 20 holes en route to a final round 65. For the second year in a row, Palmer had broken 280, making him the first man in U.S. Open history to break 280 twice. Yet he had lost both times. And as if that wasn't enough to endure, not only did Nicklaus's four-round total of 275 win the Open, it broke Ben Hogan's U.S. Open record that Palmer had been chasing at Olympic the year before.

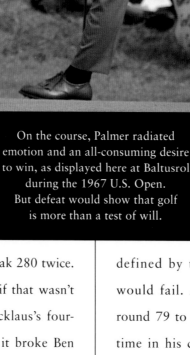

On the course, Palmer radiated emotion and an all-consuming desire to win, as displayed here at Baltusrol during the 1967 U.S. Open. But defeat would show that golf is more than a test of will.

In August, Palmer won the American Golf Classic. The victory was the 50th of his pro career, and served as a double-milestone in that it made him the first golfer in history with earnings in excess of $1 million. A month later, he added to both totals with a $30,000 triumph in the Thunderbird Classic. But again, for the third consecutive year, there was no "major" championship. And as 1967 came to an end, although Palmer had won $184,065, Nicklaus stood at $188,988. Thus, it was understandable that, when asked to assess the new crop of players on the PGA Tour, Palmer answered simply, "I see no new Nicklauses; thank God."

Like the previous two seasons, 1968 began with a good first month for Palmer. He won the Bob Hope Desert Classic and finished second at the Los Angeles Open. But again, his year would be defined by the "majors"; and once more, he would fail. At the Masters, he shot a second-round 79 to miss the cut at Augusta for the first time in his career. "I can't explain what I was doing," he told the press afterward. "But I wasn't concentrating; I wasn't on the golf course. I was

"*I remember the Thunderbird Classic in 1967. Palmer was in the clubhouse with the lead, and some guy with a walkie-talkie came in to report on the rest of the field. Billy Casper was in second place, and all Palmer asked was, 'Where's Jack?' 'Don't worry,' the guy told him. 'Jack's out of it.' Then, maybe 10 minutes later, the same guy came back and announced, 'Casper blew up; you've got it.' And Palmer said, 'Yeah, but where's Jack?' So the guy goes out, comes back a few minutes later, and says, 'Jack's on a roll; he's one stroke back.' At which point Darrell Brown, who was Palmer's pilot, asks, 'Arnie, do you want another Coke?' And Palmer, who's getting the golf balls out of his bag for a playoff, answers, 'No, I want to go home.' Then the guy with the walkie-talkie comes back a third time and says, 'Nicklaus is on the green at 18; he's putting for a birdie.' Palmer gets up, and starts to pace back and forth. And all of a sudden the guy who's talking into the walkie-talkie shouts, 'He missed it! He blew it! Nicklaus blew the putt!' And I'll never forget this. Palmer looked right at him and said, 'Ask again.'*"

JERRY IZENBERG

Palmer could only stand and watch as Nicklaus roared to victory at the
1967 U.S. Open with a record-breaking score of 275.

somewhere else." Then, at the U.S. Open, Palmer finished 59th with a 301 that included a third-round 79. The Open showcased the emergence of Lee Trevino, who matched Nicklaus's 275 of the previous year to win by four strokes. Meanwhile, all Palmer could say when it was over was, "I did everything but stand on my head out there. I didn't give a damn, and that didn't work. So I gave a damn, and that didn't work. I changed my grip; I changed my stance. Nothing helped."

In July, Palmer finished a disappointing 10th in the British Open. Then he journeyed to San Antonio for the PGA Championship, the only "major" he'd never won. For 71 holes in the heart of Texas, Arnie's Army thought its general was in command again. But on the 72nd green, he missed an eight-foot birdie putt to finish second, one stroke behind Julius Boros. And at year's end, the statistics told another frustrating story. Palmer had won two tournaments: the Bob Hope Desert Classic and Kemper Open. But he'd fallen to seventh place on the official earnings list and 21st in average strokes per round.

1969 began with a twist that sprang from changes in the structure of the game. The United States Golf Association had long been the governing body of golf insofar as the rules of play were concerned. But outside of running the U.S. Open, the

Arnold's victory at the 1968 Bob Hope Desert Classic was a rare bright spot in what was otherwise a frustrating year.

USGA had little connection to the pro tour. That was run by the PGA of America, which was comprised of touring pros and several thousand club professionals. Then, in 1968, the touring pros rebelled. They'd come to feel that the PGA was administratively inept and unresponsive to their needs. They wanted to run their own affairs. And when the PGA refused their demand for autonomy, the pros had announced the formation of an organization known as the American Professional Golfers, designed to operate a new tour. Eventually, the PGA relented and agreed to the creation of a special 10-person Tournament Policy Board. The pros' incipient organization was abandoned, and the PGA Tour became a separate entity within the PGA. 1969 was the first season played under this new regime. But for Palmer, the results were more of the same.

The greatest indication of how far Palmer had fallen lay in the fact that, for the first time in 10 years, he was forced to enter a qualifying tournament before being admitted to the U.S. Open. Players were automatically eligible for the Open if they'd won either the Open or PGA within the preceding five years, were the current U.S. Amateur or British Open champion, finished in the top 15 at the previous Open, or were among the year's top 15 PGA money winners at the time entries were due for the current Open. Palmer met none of those

"*Arnold knocked the ball way into the rough, into a pile of twigs and leaves. I think there was a dead squirrel and a beer can in there too. Anyway, he walked over and stared down at his ball. And then he saw me standing there and asked, 'Okay, wiseguy. What would your idol, Hogan, do here?' And I told him, 'Hogan wouldn't be here.'*"

JIM MURRAY

standards. "I can't really object to qualifying," he said after getting out of bed at 4:50 a.m. and shooting rounds of 70 and 68 to lead 52 golfers who were competing for eight slots. "If I was running the USGA and you asked me if I'd make a man of my position qualify, I'd say no. But if the ruling body says this is the right way, who am I to protest? These are the rules."

In the end, in one of those inexplicable quirks of fate, the 1969 Open belonged to a career Army sergeant named Orville Moody, who fired a 281 for the first and only regular PGA tour victory of his career. Palmer finished three strokes back. And as the season progressed, he could do no better than third in any of 24 tournaments he entered. Meanwhile, on September 10th, his 40th birthday, the tributes had a poignant note. "He first came to golf as a muscular young man who hit the ball with all the finesse of a dock worker lifting a crate of auto parts," Dan Jenkins wrote. "He made birdies by driving through forests, lacing hooks around sharp corners, spewing wild slices over prodigious hills, and staring putts into the cup. His method seemed to be, 'hit it hard, go find it, and hit it hard again.' And he became a winner like none we had ever known." And then Jenkins closed his

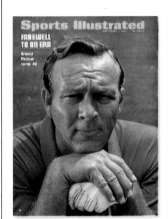

"Thanks for the Memories" ran the headline in *Sports Illustrated*'s tribute to Palmer on his 40th birthday: "Perhaps never again will there be a golfer with the universal appeal of Arnold Palmer. For more than a decade he has been a classic hero: bold, reckless, ever foolhardy – traits that have cost him titles at times but have won him the admiration of the world."

piece with the thought, "Hell, Arnold. Lately, you've even given a nobility to losing."

So all Palmer did at the end of 1969 was go out and win the last two tournaments of the year. His victory at the Heritage Classic was his first in 14 months. And at the Danny Thomas-Diplomat Classic, he carded a final-round 65 to rally from six strokes back and become the only golfer with back-to-back triumphs on the pro tour that season. Thus, the 1960s ended as they'd begun; with Arnold Palmer on a roll. And to further validate his accomplishments, an Associated Press poll of 655 broadcasters and sportswriters named him "Athlete of the Decade." "I'm overwhelmed that they chose me, but it's much more than that," Palmer said on learning of the award. "To think that a golfer would be chosen is fantastic." And as if to justify its faith, Arnie's Army entered 1970 with a new battle cry – "Life begins at 40!" After all, Ben Hogan's greatest triumphs had come in 1953 when, at age 40, he'd won the Masters, U.S. Open, and British Open. But Hogan had played a different game from Palmer.

Arnold's popularity continued unabated in 1970. At times, he seemed omnipresent in the world of advertising. He even substituted for

Johnny Carson as host of "The Tonight Show," with Spiro Agnew and Vic Damone as his guests. But for the first time in his pro career, he failed to win an individual tournament. "It seems that every day I start out with great expectations, and then it's the same old problem," Palmer said, explaining his woes. "I've had some good streaks, but there's something missing from my putting. I don't feel nervous or jumpy. But I look at the hole and have absolutely no idea where the ball is going. I know where I want it to go, but I'm not making it go there. I'm optimistic enough to think that I'll recover it at some point, but I haven't had it in a long time. I'd like to think it's something that will come back when I'm 41."

And remarkably, it did. 1971 was Palmer's best season in four years. In February, he birdied the first hole of a sudden-death playoff against Raymond Floyd to win the Bob Hope Desert Classic. "You know what a struggle this has been," he told reporters after his second 14-month victory drought in two-and-a-half years. "I looked at people who were following me, and some of them were crying. I said, 'Why are you crying

"You can't swing freely if your muscles are tense. You can't putt if your muscles are tense. Yet when a golfer is under pressure, the tension is there."

ARNOLD PALMER

when I win? You should cry when I get beat.' I still can't understand why my winning seems to give other people so much pleasure, but I'm glad they feel that way about me."

In March, Palmer won again; this time at the Florida Citrus Open. That win was significant anecdotally because an avid fan followed Arnold around the course while he shot a second-round 68 and determined that, over the course of 18 holes, he'd hitched up his pants 345 times. "My belief is that hitching my pants is a way of preventing tension from growing," Palmer explained afterward. "On the other hand, there is a reason that my nervous release involves hitching. When I was a boy, my pants kept sliding down, and my mother was always saying, 'Arnold, pull up your pants and tuck your shirt in.' So I started hitching up then, and I've never stopped."

"Arnold seems to have mellowed enough to realize that he's not going to win every week," Mark McCormack said of his client's rejuvenation. "And that attitude has made him a winner again." Meanwhile, Palmer had his own explanation. "It makes all the difference in the world when the putts are dropping," he said. And at the Westchester Classic, they continued to drop. Starting with an opening-round 64, Palmer led after all four days, won by five strokes, and finished at 18 under par to break the tournament record by two strokes. Next, he and Jack Nicklaus joined to capture the PGA Team Championship. By year's end, Arnold had won $209,603 in tour earnings, the highest total of his career, and everything seemed to be going right. But then, in 1972, the fates conspired to remind him of just how difficult it was for a 42-year-old man to succeed on the PGA Tour.

Back in 1958, Palmer had observed, "The trouble with golf is that as you learn more, you get older and you start to lose out physically and in concentration. If there was a way you could stay young for 30 years and keep learning all that time, you might have a perfect golfer." But no athlete stays young forever, and Palmer's style was particularly vulnerable to age. "Arnold did not have a good swing," sports-marketing executive Barry Frank recalls. "He drove the ball well, but his swing was flat so that he'd finish with his hands out in front of him instead of behind. And when you swing that hard with that kind of swing,

A bespectacled Palmer was faced with the reality that athletes grow old before their time.

a lot of things can go wrong. Think of the effect that being an eighth-of-an-inch off has on a trajectory of 250 yards, and you'll understand what happened when Arnold lost a bit of his coordination. And on top of that, as he got older it became harder for him to compensate for his shortcomings with brute strength. He was never a great chipper; and as he started to fall short of the greens, that part of his game became more of a problem."

Also, Byron Nelson adds, "Everyone's putting deteriorates when he gets older. Your sense of balance isn't the same. Your muscular sensitivity is different, and your eyesight changes. It's not that you can't see the ball or the condition of the green, but there's a difference in the keenness of the eye. That's why the armed forces use young men to fly. And either a golfer accepts the fact that his putting isn't as good as it used to be, or he quits."

Palmer didn't quit. But in 1972, it must have seemed to him as though the fairways were getting longer and the holes smaller. And like most people in their mid-40s, he was having trouble with his eyes. In Arnold's case, the problem was nearsightedness. As early as 1971, he recalls, "I became aware that I couldn't quite see where the ball was dropping on some of the long tee shots. It was just fading into the fuzzy distance. And at about the same time, I discovered that I couldn't always see and measure from the fairway just where the pin was placed on a particular green." Palmer went to an optometrist and learned that his eyesight was 20/50 in one eye and 20/30 in the other. In mid-1971, he began to wear eyeglasses in practice, but complained, "They slip when I bend down; they hurt behind the ears; they steam up; things like that." Then he was fitted for a pair of soft contact lenses. And when he began 1972 with his worst start in 16 years, he decided to wear the lenses in competition.

The "new" Arnold Palmer made his debut at the Greensboro Open, and finished third at 273. That was promising. But a week later at Augusta, he logged his worst score in 18 years of Masters play – a final-round 81 en route to 33rd place – while Jack Nicklaus won his fourth Masters crown. Then, on the first day at the Tournament of Champions, Arnold's eyes became irritated after 15 holes, so he removed his contact lenses and finished the round wearing regular glasses. The next two days, he wore neither lenses nor glasses. And then he wore lenses again during the final round. "I'm trying to wear contact lenses; I'm wearing glasses; I really

"I remember being in Toots Shor's one Saturday night. Arnold was leading the Westchester Classic after three rounds, and there he was, at one o'clock in the morning, drinking scotch like he didn't have a thing to do the following afternoon. I don't mean he was drunk; he wasn't. But he was enjoying himself. Part of Arnold's charm was he always knew how to have a good time."

JACK MEYERS

don't know what I'm wearing," Palmer said when the tournament was done. "When I wear contacts, I see a lot better; and I feel a lot better on the golf course when I'm looking at something. But on a windy day or a heavy pollen day, you have problems with contacts; they bother you. I'm trying to find something that will give me that little extra I need to see to play as well as I can. I don't know. Maybe I'll just try to make my eyes work a little better for me. That may be the answer. It's just one of those periods I've had through the years. Everybody goes through these things in a lifetime." Still, age was creeping up on Arnold. "I'm 42 years old," he acknowledged. "I'm not going to try to birdie the world anymore."

In June, Palmer gathered himself for another try at the U.S. Open crown. His quest began poorly with an opening-round 77. But then he carded a second-round 68, the lowest score recorded by anyone during the tournament, to move into contention. A third-day 73 left him only two strokes behind Jack Nicklaus on the leaderboard. And a 40-foot birdie putt on the third hole of the final round narrowed Jack's lead to one. But that was as close as Arnold could get. Nicklaus won his third U.S. Open title – the 13th "major" championship of his career, tying him with Bobby Jones.

And Palmer's year remained unfulfilled. His $84,181 in purses left him 25th on the earnings list; far behind Jack's $320,542. And more significantly, for the first time in his pro career, he had failed to win a tournament of any kind.

"What the hell," Palmer said when 1972 was done. "It was bound to happen sometime. All I can do is go out and try to win the first thing in 1973." But 1973 began with a 24th place finish at the Los Angeles Open, followed by 49th- and 22nd-place showings. To many, it seemed like wishful thinking for Arnold to contemplate winning again. Yet there was one more official tour victory left in him.

It came on February 11, 1973, at the Bob Hope Desert Classic; a tournament Palmer had won on four previous occasions. The Hope was different from most PGA tournaments in that it was played over four different courses and totalled 90 holes. Nicklaus took the early lead, and held it through four rounds. Then, on day five, he and Palmer were paired together, and Arnold overcame a two-stroke deficit to lead by two going to the par-5 final hole. There, the drama grew more intense. Nicklaus was on the green in two, 30 feet

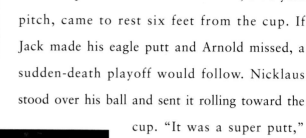

Palmer celebrates his last tour victory, after a birdie putt on the final hole of the 1973 Bob Hope Desert Classic defeats his arch-rival, second-place finisher Jack Nicklaus.

from the pin. And Palmer's third shot, a 50-yard pitch, came to rest six feet from the cup. If Jack made his eagle putt and Arnold missed, a sudden-death playoff would follow. Nicklaus stood over his ball and sent it rolling toward the cup. "It was a super putt," Palmer remembers. "I thought he'd made it." But Jack was off by a fraction of an inch, and Palmer sealed the victory with a birdie putt of his own.

Four months later, there was equal drama when the U.S. Open returned to the Oakmont Country Club, where 11 years earlier, "Arnie versus Jack" had been born. A lot had happened in those 11 years. In 1962, the prevailing view had been that Palmer might become the greatest golfer of all time. Now that designation was far more likely to be spoken in conjunction with Nicklaus's name. But beyond that, Jack had begun to remake himself in what many believed was the image of Arnold Palmer. He'd gone on a diet and lost 25 pounds, including six inches from his hips. His hair had grown long; even the shape of his face seemed to have changed. And equally important, Nicklaus had begun to open up more and laugh at himself. Recalling a comment by Jim Murray that he looked "not

"Ask any athlete who has thrown a block, sunk a free throw, hit a curve ball, and tried to play golf. Nine times out of 10, they'll tell you that nothing in sports is as scary as a seven-foot putt you have to make."

DICK SCHAAP

so much like an athlete as a pile of old clothes," Jack remarked, "I finally met Jim Murray at a banquet; he was fatter than I was." And after four-putting on national television, Nicklaus observed, "That fourth putt was a beauty; it went right smack in the center of the cup."

Thus, the 1973 Open represented a strange walk back in time. An aging but ever-popular "Arnie" versus the "Golden Bear" in his prime. It was an opportunity for "poetic justice"; a chance for Arnold to remedy all those "almosts" that had gone wrong. And Palmer gave it his best shot. At age 43, in the toughest tournament in the world, he was tied for first after three rounds. But then Johnny Miller fired a record-breaking 63 to claim the U.S. Open crown.

Palmer never came as close to winning a "major" again, and his play in general continued to decline. "I don't care if I'm the sentimental favorite," he said in 1974. "I just want to win myself a golf tournament." Still, that year, he could do no better than fifth place in any PGA tournament, and he dropped to 72nd on the tour earnings list. In 1976, he ranked 115th; and in 1977, for the first time in his career, he failed to record a top-10 finish in any regular tour event.

ARNOLD PALMER

Palmer in the cockpit of his
Jet Commander, 1967.

Yet through it all, he was able to proclaim, "Life is super; I'm healthy; I'm happy. You might not believe this, but I think I enjoy playing now more than I ever did. In the old days, everything seemed to be such a necessity. There wasn't much I could treat casually. But now I really enjoy everything. The only thing is, I'd like to be playing like I did 20 years ago; but I guess everyone my age would."

Meanwhile, as Palmer's golf game became less sure, he continued to derive gratification from other endeavors. His business life grew even more active than before. And in 1976, he joined a three-man team seeking to circumnavigate the globe in world-record time for jets in the 17,600- to 26,400-pound category. Arnold loved aviation. "It started when I was a little boy," he explained. "If there was anything that could compete with my interest in golf, it was flying. When I wasn't building model planes, I was running down the country club road to the airport, where some of the pilots would gather around an old pot-bellied stove; and I'd just sit there listening to all the glories of the sky."

Palmer had taken his first flying lessons in 1956, and began soloing two years later. Then he realized it would be cost efficient to have his own plane for expanded business activity and to avoid the hassle of traveling from tournament to tournament by trailer or on regularly scheduled flights. In 1960, he bought a second-hand six-seat twin-engine Aero Commander 500. Three years later, that was upgraded to an Aero Commander 560F. And in 1966, he leased his first jet, a Rockwell-Standard Corporation Jet Commander, at what the manufacturer termed "a substantial discount off retail" in return for appearing in advertisements for the plane. "If it wasn't for flying, I wouldn't be playing golf today," Arnold quipped in 1965. "I loathe driving 2,000 miles every Monday."

Palmer's 1976 around-the-world venture was undertaken in a red-white-and-blue Learjet 36 as part of America's year-long Bicentennial celebration. Two co-pilots, James Bir and Bill Purkey, and Bob Serling, an observer-timer representing the National Aeronautic Association, joined him. "It's something I'll get a big kick out of," Arnold told a press conference the day before the flight. "I'm doing this for the excitement of it, and just because I want to. The element of risk has been reduced to the near-vanishing point, but the adventure is still there."

As part of America's 1976 Bicentennial celebration, Palmer and two co-pilots circumnavigated the globe in world-record time in their Learjet 36, Freedom's Way U.S.A.

The 22,984-mile undertaking began at Denver's Stapleton International Airport on May 17, 1976, at 10:24 a.m. Palmer and company landed for refueling in Boston, Paris, Tehran, Sri Lanka, Jakarta, Manila, Wake Island, and Honolulu.

At each stop, the crew gave American Bicentennial flags and a bronze replica of the Declaration of Independence to representatives of the host country. "At times, it got a little lonely," Arnold remembers. "Especially the night I was flying over the Indian Ocean. It was overcast, so there was no moon or stars, and I had some trouble with the navigational equipment. The other guys were asleep, and I began to wonder, 'What in hell am I doing here?' I don't recommend that you fly an airplane over the Indian Ocean to get insight into yourself, but it was a tremendous experience."

The flight touched down in Denver on May 19th at 7:49 p.m. The old record, set 10 years earlier, had been 86 hours 9 minutes. Boosted by advances in aviation technology, Palmer, Bir and Purkey had shattered that mark with a new standard of 57 hours 25 minutes 42 seconds. "It wasn't that great a feat," Arnold said afterward. "But it isn't done every day." And as a *Time* magazine dispatch noted, "Considering the water hazards and long pars, the 46-year-old Palmer didn't do a bad job. He was 77-1/2 days ahead of Phileas Fogg."

Subsequent to his around-the-world flight, Palmer returned to the PGA Tour. But as Joe Falls wrote, the time had come to view him, "not as a potential champion, but as a beautiful man who has done so much for the game that we should all be glad he's still around." There were flashes of brilliance now and then. A 32 on the front nine of round one at the 1980 U.S. Open; a 68 in the opening round of the 1983 Masters. But the birdies were coming far less often with many more holes in between.

On four occasions, the USGA gave Palmer a "special exemption" to play in the U.S. Open; and twice more, he qualified on his own. Then, in 1984, the exemption was withheld, and Arnold came up two strokes short at a sectional qualifying tournament on the outskirts of Cleveland. That ended a string of 31 consecutive U.S. Open appearances – a record he shared with Gene Sarazen. The same year, he was unable to make the cut at any of the other

Inaugural inductee Arnold Palmer addresses an assembly at the World Golf Hall of Fame dedication ceremony in Pinehurst, North Carolina, September, 1974.

three "majors." And in 1985, at age 55, Palmer announced his "semi-retirement" from the regular PGA Tour. Thereafter, he continued to play, although in fewer tournaments than before, and the galleries loved him just the same. As far as Arnie's Army was concerned, their general never lost a tournament; he just ran out of holes to play.

"Losing never diminished Arnold's mystique," Pat Summerall says, looking back on it all. "All it did was change the aura that surrounded him from one of expectancy to one of hope. When he was young, you expected him to outdrive every other golfer, hit every green, make every putt, and win every tournament. And then, when the transition came, you simply hoped the magic would return, maybe for a round or two, so you could catch a glimpse of the old Arnie again." "I'll tell you something," adds Dave Marr, "On top of everything else, Arnold turned out to be bulletproof. He can shoot an 85 today, and people still love him."

Arnold Palmer didn't just make fans on the golf course. He kept them for life.

"I'd rather win one tournament in my life than make the cut every week."

ARNOLD PALMER

Nobody ever hit a ball with his reputation.

"The golf ball doesn't appreciate that you're a hot shot player, nor does the course. It's a clean sheet every time you play, and you have to impress them with your talent all over again."
Arnold Palmer

Unlike any other golfer, Palmer needed
state troopers to move him through the crowds.

Facing page: At the 1967 U.S. Open;
another victory for Nicklaus and a heartbreaking loss for Palmer.

"Golf is the most challenging game a man can play. And it's a game you have to constantly think about and work at, depending on how important the game is to you and how well you want to play. If you want to do less, you can get away with less as long as the game doesn't matter to you. But if you're really into playing well, golf is as demanding a challenge as any person can face."

ARNOLD PALMER

A second-round 79 prevented Palmer from making the cut at the 1968 Masters.

Palmer's personalized shag bag from the early 1980s.

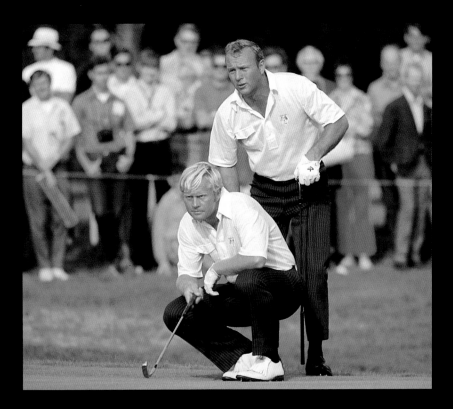

Palmer with Ryder Cup teammates Jack Nicklaus in 1971 (above)
and Lee Trevino and Tom Weiskopf in 1975 (below).

*"The spirit and camaraderie of players coming out of competition with each other and teaming up
against a common foe at the Ryder Cup was a remarkable experience for me."*

ARNOLD PALMER

"*Nobody loves golf more than Arnold. Look at what he's done for the sport. The American press was inclined to forget that golf was played in other parts of the world. And by going to St. Andrews, Arnold almost single-handedly returned the British Open to its rightful position of grandeur. He's our foremost ambassador to the world, and the international symbol of excellence in golf.*"

GARY PLAYER

Arnold at Carnoustie during the 1968 British Open.

*"Some people think of me as just plain lucky. I can't argue with them.
I would like to say, however, that a man might be walking around lucky
and not know it unless he tries."*

Arnold Palmer

Diamond-studded honorary Captain's "Wings"
presented to Palmer by United Airlines.

*"Jack and I had just played the last round of the Bob Hope Desert Classic together.
And afterward, everybody went to a jam session at Indian Wells. Jack got there before I did.
He was sitting at the same table I sat at every year with some of my friends. I walked in;
they waved for me to join them. I started back toward the table; and as I did, I bumped against
a lady who was sitting at another table and knocked her wig off her head. Her hair was in curlers;
she was terribly embarrassed. And to draw attention away from her and help avoid further
embarrassment, I picked up the wig and put it on my head. Everybody got a big kick out of that.
Then I looked back toward the table where I was heading, and Jack threw me a kiss, so I asked
him to dance. Anyway, Jack got up and came to the dance floor, so I knew I was in trouble.
And that's when I took the wig off and put it on his head."*

ARNOLD PALMER

*"It was at a jam session at Indian Wells. I had to get up to go to the bathroom.
And on the way, I walked by this lady and knocked her wig off by accident.
And as I remember, I picked the wig up, put it on Arnold's head, and led him out to dance.
Then he put it on my head, and we danced some more. We laughed and it was kind of fun,
although the lady whose wig it was didn't think it was all that funny."*

JACK NICKLAUS

*"I don't know who asked who to dance first. But if I remember that picture correctly,
they both looked like they were having a pretty good time."*

SAM SNEAD

"Over the years, the beauty of golf courses has remained unchanged.
Dome stadiums have turned football from a game that was profoundly influenced by
nature into one where it can be zero degrees outside and the weather doesn't matter.
Baseball has adopted artificial turf, which alters the way the game is played.
Boxing paints beer company logos on its ring canvases.
But golf's playing fields are still unspoiled and clean."

ARNOLD PALMER

Above: Palmer at the Masters, 1984 (top) and 1988.
Facing page: Palmer at the inaugural made-for-TV Skins Game
at the Nicklaus-designed Desert Highlands in 1983.

Part Five

Arnold Palmer's America

This Masters Trophy, a silver replica of the Augusta National Clubhouse, was presented to Palmer for his victories in 1958, 1960, 1962 and 1964.

It's noon on a warm December day. The sky is blue, and a gentle breeze

is playing with the trees. At the Bay Hill Club in Orlando, Florida, two dozen men have gathered to play golf. Several are resident club pros. Others are corporate executives on vacation at Bay Hill or retirees who live there during the winter months. Earlier in the day, each of them dropped by the pro shop, paid $30 into a prize pool, and entered his name in the daily ritual known as "The Bay Hill Shoot-Out." Then a retired auto dealer, acting as unofficial chairman of a nonexistent tournament committee, divided the men by ability into six four-man teams. The first foursome will tee off at 12:30 p.m. Over the course of 18 holes, the best three balls scored by each team on each hole will be recorded. At day's end, the teams will be judged by comparing their number one, number two, and number three balls. With $720 in the pot, the best score in each category will be worth $240.

At 12:15, a 64-year-old man joins the others at the practice tees. His face is weathered from a lifetime of working outdoors. It's a happy face; and no matter how many lines there are around his eyes or how thin and gray his hair gets, part of him still looks like a boy. His hands are large and remarkably strong. When he speaks, it's with a western-Pennsylvania accent closer in cadence to rural Ohio than Philadelphia. And despite his age, there's an aura about him. He's in a good mood, because he's getting ready to play golf – something

Facing page: From champion to American legend.

he does almost every day when he's at home. "I love going out on a golf course," he says. "It never bores me, even if I've played the course a thousand times before." Someone asks how many strokes he might cut from his score if he plays this afternoon's round with the same intensity that he exudes in a major tournament. "I'm pretty intense right now," Arnold Palmer answers. "This is for serious money."

Arnold Palmer is pretty much where he wants to be in life these days. He and Winnie have been married for 39 years. They have two daughters in their mid-30s – Peg, who works for a printing company in Durham, North Carolina; and Amy, who owns a small gift shop in Orlando. Both daughters are married. Amy has four children; Peg one, with another on the way. From May through October, Arnold and Winnie live in Latrobe in the home they bought in 1958. Originally, it was a six-room ranch house painted white with black shutters. Over the next eight years, they converted the garage into an office, expanded the cellar, constructed a new kitchen and dining room, and enlarged the bedrooms. Then, as Palmer's business interests continued to grow, he built a separate office building 100 yards up the road. That serves

From May through October, Arnold and Winnie still live in Latrobe in the often-expanded house they purchased in 1958.

as his home-base office today, and is supervised on a daily basis by Doc Giffin.

Giffin is one of a handful of people who've been central to Palmer's life over the past quarter-century. Once a sportswriter for the *Pittsburgh Press*, he became press secretary for the PGA Tour in 1962. "Arnold was at the peak of his career," Doc recalls, "and I worked with him quite a bit. Then, in 1966, he told me his obligations had reached a point where the one secretary he had wasn't enough, and asked if I'd come to work for him. Originally, the idea was that I'd be a sort of traveling administrative assistant. But after a while, it became apparent that I could accomplish more by staying in Latrobe, and that's where I am today."

Giffin now has two secretaries and his own administrative aide. In addition to handling a never-ending stream of requests for autographs and charity-auction items, he directs business inquiries to the proper party in the Palmer corporate empire, processes media requests, and ghostwrites various articles and speeches for Arnold. "As far back as I can remember," says Amy Palmer, "Doc has been a loyal worker and friend. He's always there when Daddy needs him. At the end of most days, he comes down to the house for a drink with my parents, but he's never intruded on our personal lives." Meanwhile, the office in Latrobe keeps growing. "Ten years ago, I was sure things would be slowing down by now," says Winnie Palmer. "And instead, we've just built a new wing on the building."

Palmer has many links to Latrobe beyond the fact that he lives there for six months a year. He owns seven houses, 150 acres of unimproved hillside, and 50 acres of farmland in the area. His brother and both of his sisters live nearby. And then there's the matter of the Latrobe Country Club, where Arnold learned to play golf as a boy. The course was expanded to 18 holes in 1964, and Palmer bought it in 1971. He's now the club president, while his brother Jerry serves as general manager. Also, Winnie Palmer explains, "One of the things Arnie likes most about Latrobe is that people aren't overly impressed with his celebrity status because they've known him all his life. That's why, when someone says to us, as they often do, 'Come to Palm Desert; we'll give you a house and a million dollars to promote our development,' we say, 'No thanks; we're happy where we are.'" During the winter months, Arnold and Winnie live at Bay Hill. "We used to come to Florida for six weeks

The two golf courses owned by Palmer: Bay Hill Club (above) and Latrobe Country Club (below).

each winter so Arnie could practice," Winnie remembers. "The children came with us before they were old enough to go to school. And later on, we were fortunate to have two sets of healthy loving parents who took care of them while we were gone. Then one day, Arnie came to me and said, 'Babe, I've just seen the best golf course in all Florida, and I want it.' I've never forgotten that moment."

Neither has Arnold. "It was a 1965 exhibition at Bay Hill," he recalls. "I shot a 65, and it was one of the best courses I'd ever been on. Most of the area was wilderness then. There were orange groves, rattlesnakes and quail all over the place. The club had a pro shop and a couple of cottages; that's all. And I wanted to be there. Essentially, I was looking for a self-supporting club where I could live during the winter months and play golf with my friends. It was a question of lifestyle; not an investment. I couldn't afford to buy the place then. But from 1965 through 1969, Mark McCormack and I negotiated with the owners; and in 1969, we closed a deal on a lease with an option to buy. Then, in 1972, Disney World opened; Orlando took off; and from a business perspective, our agenda changed. Disney screwed up my plans for a quiet

"*I suppose in some ways Daddy has mellowed in recent years. And I think he's been able to enjoy my children more than he enjoyed Peg and me, because he has more time now to spend with family. But he's still basically the same person he always was; he just shows it differently.*"

AMY PALMER SAUNDERS

Palmer's morning ritual at Latrobe sees him up at 5:00 a.m.,
exercise, breakfast and at the office by 8:00.

out-of-the-way place to play golf, but it was great for our investment."

Palmer is now president and principal owner of the 200-acre Bay Hill Club and Lodge. Unlike the Latrobe Country Club, which is a small seasonal family golf club, Bay Hill involves running a hotel, tennis courts, and a very busy golf course for 12 months a year. Arnold and Winnie own a condominium on the club grounds. Like their home in Latrobe, it's remarkably modest, given Palmer's enormous financial holdings. But as Winnie explains, "Arnie is very frugal. And because of the way I was raised, instead of letting his financial success go to my head and buying everything I could get my hands on the way many young wives do today, I've encouraged that frugality. Both of us were raised to save and be ready for worse times. Obviously, we've been very fortunate in that times have just kept getting better for us, but we helped make that happen. We never lived beyond our means. We always paid for what we bought when we bought it and never went into debt. We never felt a desire to be showy, and still don't."

Thus, the only true luxury item that Arnold owns today is his Cessna Citation VII jet. Both

"As long as Arnold Palmer is playing golf, the rest of us can pretend we're not old."

JIM MURRAY

Palmer homes are tastefully decorated, but the most valuable work of art in either of them is a pastoral scene that hangs in the Palmer living room in Latrobe; a painting given to Arnold by the artist, Dwight Eisenhower, at a surprise birthday party in 1966. And Palmer follows a daily routine that mirrors what he likes to do in life.

"Arnie and I are early risers in the morning and quick finishers at night," Winnie says, framing their day. "We get up around five a.m., and Arnie does his exercises. He has just the hint of a back problem, and the doctor told him that, if he does stretching exercises faithfully for the rest of his life, it should be all right. So he does those and some stationary bicycle riding and works with some other exercise equipment while I'm showering, dressing, and making breakfast. Sometimes Arnie eats, and then shaves and showers. Sometimes it's the other way around. Either way, he's at the office by eight and works until noon. Then he has a bowl of soup, goes out and plays golf, has a beer in the locker room, and comes home. We enjoy a few drinks and have dinner together. In Latrobe, most of the time we eat at home. At Bay Hill, we're more likely to go over to the club for dinner. Afterward, if there's time, Arnie might turn on the television. Then, around 9:30, we go to bed. And once his head hits the pillow, he's gone."

When Palmer has free time, he's likely to spend it working with his golf clubs. By most estimates, he has the largest private collection in the world; roughly 7,000 clubs in Latrobe and 3,000 more in Florida. "The majority of them are putters," Doc Giffin elaborates. "For 30 years, every time there's been a story in the newspapers about how Arnold's putting isn't what he'd like it to be, he gets a slew of putters in the mail. Some are fluky-type things, putters you wouldn't dream of using. But Arnold will hit a few balls with almost anything that's sent to him, even if he doesn't use it in an actual round. Most of the irons and woods are from his own company, which he's had in one

form or another since the early 1960s. Some are from other manufacturers who want him to try their equipment. And of course, he's kept almost all the clubs he's ever used in tournament play."

But Palmer is far from content just owning golf clubs. He's constantly reshaping them in workshops located in a back room of his Latrobe office and beneath his condominium at Bay Hill. One often-told tale recalls an incident in 1960,

when Arnold borrowed a driver from Ben Hogan. In Palmer's words, "It was exactly what I wanted. With just a small change here and there, I built up the grip a bit and made it slightly shorter. I put a little more loft on the face of the clubhead and a little bit of a gooseneck into it. I sanded and refinished it." And legend has it that, when Hogan next saw his club, he demanded in horror, "What have you done to my driver? You've ruined a perfectly good club."

Be that as it may, Palmer acknowledges, "I guess I'm a pro's son at heart. My father taught me every detail about how to work in the shop, building and rebuilding clubs, adding weights under the plate, changing the shafts and grips, finishing and refinishing. I call it constructive relaxation. And it's probably just a personal idiosyncrasy, but I've never had a bag of clubs I've been completely satisfied with." To which Winnie adds, "Arnie has an obsession with making the perfect set of golf clubs. He probably spends more time whittling and fiddling and regripping and reweighting and regluing than anything else in life. He even has a traveling case of drills and files, so he can do it wherever we go. And sometimes it drives me to total distraction, because I can't believe he's capable of redoing a particular club one more time."

For the most part, Palmer's other personal habits are unremarkable. "If we're listening to music, he likes big bands from the '40s and '50s," Winnie reports. "On television, it's old westerns, the news, "Murder, She Wrote," and anything related to golf. As far as movies are concerned, he likes westerns with lots of shooting and noise. Arnie's a real cowboy at heart. In fact, I think he wants to be reincarnated and come back in his next life as John Wayne. And it's very important to him that the good guys win at the end of a movie. He's moralistic about that sort of thing. In sports, he roots for the Pittsburgh teams: the Pirates, the Steelers and the Penguins. He doesn't care about tennis. And last year he took me to an Orlando Magic basketball game because the Chicago Bulls were in town and I wanted to see Michael Jordan."

Palmer was raised as a Lutheran, and belongs to a Presbyterian church in Latrobe. Occasionally, he and Winnie go to Methodist services in Orlando. But except for Christmas, he's not a regular churchgoer. He seldom reads except for business, and hasn't smoked since the early 1970s. He loves to fly, and gets almost as much pleasure today from aviation as from golf. He's unfailingly courteous with waitresses,

"In 1980, I was with Arnold at a tournament in Palm Springs. And out of the blue, Arnold said to me, 'I've got an idea; I think I should make western movies. I can ride a horse; I can handle a gun. I'd be a great star.' I thought he was kidding, but he wasn't because the next day he asked, 'Did you think any more about that idea of me being in westerns?' And for two or three days, he was serious about it. He really wanted to be a western star. And knowing Arnold, and keeping in mind that he's my client, I think he'd have been great."

BARRY FRANK

doormen, and everyone else he comes in contact with, and specializes in gracious gestures like a friendly wink or quick smile to make awkward fans feel at ease. And his patience with fans is extraordinary. To some, that's a bit incongruous since, as Winnie once said, "At home, the one thing Arnie is not, is a very patient man." But the fact remains that Palmer has a personal policy of shaking hands and giving autographs no matter how tired he is on a given day. That can be a demanding chore. Palmer rarely gets to finish a meal in a restaurant without interruption. At tournaments, he's besieged by fans who shove pens in his face and grab at his arms. Yet he virtually never shows annoyance, because as his brother Jerry explains, "Arnie likes to be liked, and wants everybody in the world to feel they're his friend. Obviously, there are times when that can be difficult. You have to understand what it's like to go through life every day with hundreds of people pulling on you, tugging at you, wanting autographs, handshakes, business deals, charity donations; and to have a code that requires you to be kind and courteous to everyone and disappoint as few people as possible. But Arnie does it, and that's one of the reasons all of us in the family are so proud of him."

Palmer for his part says simply, "It irritates me when people are rude. Every person has a right to get angry and display his feelings, but I believe we all have an obligation to treat other people the way we'd like to be treated. There are times when I'm out, and I'd rather have a drink by myself without someone I've never met coming by to say hello. But most of the people I meet are friendly. And quite frankly, I like people. So if I don't want to chat with strangers, I stay home. If I feel that what I'm doing is a burden, I just quit doing it. Sure, there are times when I say to myself that I'd like to have everything I have today without being famous. But that's impossible, because many of the very good things that have happened to me in life have come about because I am known around the world. So I can't sit here and say I'd like to own this and do that and not have the hassles of fame, because it all goes together. And if I'm being honest with myself, part of me enjoys being famous. I'd have to enjoy it to some degree to do what I do."

Palmer is used to controlling his world. He hits a golf ball, and it's all up to him. He flies a plane, and it's all in his hands. He's one of those lucky few who seems to have lived his life almost

Palmer won the first event he entered on the PGA Senior Tour – the 1980 PGA Seniors Championship.

precisely the way he wants. "I suppose Arnie was happiest in the early 1960s when he was winning the most," Winnie says, reflecting on it all. "He had so much confidence in himself back then. And we were young enough and naive enough not to be scared. But even though Arnie doesn't play as well now as he used to, life is still wonderful for both of us. And in many ways, we're more secure now than we were before."

Palmer spends roughly fifty percent of his time today in Latrobe or Orlando and the other half on the road. In addition to extensive business travel, he competes in approximately 26 tournaments a year – most of them on golf's Senior Tour. The senior circuit began in 1980, and is open to players age 50 and over. Arnold won the first seniors event he entered – the 1980 PGA Seniors Championship – and has prevailed in 11 more since then. "From tee to green, Arnold is still as good as any seniors player out there," says Lee Trevino. "He hits it a heck of a lot longer than I do, and a lot of his shots are more accurate than mine. Where we get Arnold is on the greens."

Palmer has also excelled in several versions of the made-for-TV "Skins Game." In the first such outing in 1983, competing against Jack Nicklaus,

Gary Player, and Tom Watson, he rolled in a 40-foot birdie putt on the 12th hole for $100,000, giving him $140,000 for the two-day event. But those numbers pale by comparison with Arnold's earnings from victories in three of the last five "senior skins" competitions against Nicklaus, Player, Trevino, Chi-Chi Rodriguez, and Raymond Floyd. Those victories were worth $635,000.

"Thanks to my new hearing aid, I can hear the click of my club against the ball again. Unfortunately, I heard it click 77 times today."

ARNOLD PALMER

Palmer still appears occasionally on the regular PGA Tour. The Nestle Invitational is held annually at Bay Hill, and he's always a participant. He's a regular at the Bob Hope Desert Classic. And lifetime exemptions allow him to play each year in the Masters and PGA Championship. The last time Palmer made the cut at a "major" was at the PGA in 1989. But as Byron Nelson observes, "Arnold still plays a pretty good game of golf. I don't know anyone else who's 64 who can beat him." And Palmer himself explains, "I play golf because I enjoy the challenge and because it makes me feel alive. I miss being able to do some of the things on a golf course that were once relatively easy for me. But when the talk turns to retirement, I start thinking about what I'd do. I like to fly; I do that now. I like to work on my golf clubs, and I do that now. I thoroughly enjoy playing golf, and I do that now. I like to practice, and I still do that. I read a little from time to time. Occasionally Winnie makes me go to a movie. So what would I do if I retired? What am I going to do that I don't do now, and would I enjoy it any more than I enjoy what I'm doing now?"

Thus, Palmer continues to do what he likes to do, and a lot of that centers on his business empire. With a net worth in the mid-eight figures, he's long past the point where he works out of financial necessity. But like most successful businessmen, he enjoys the chase. "Arnold loves being a tycoon," says Barry Frank. "He loves the concept of Arnold Palmer, executive, flying from country to country. He loves the fact that he has endorsement contracts for non-golf-related products with umpteen different companies. And I think one of the reasons he enjoys it so much is because it's so distant from anything he dared dream about when he was growing up as the greenskeeper's son." "I think Daddy works as hard as he does today because he's afraid not to," adds Amy Palmer. "It's past the point where he works to provide for the family. But his father always worked as hard as he could, and Daddy is driven. He wouldn't know what to do with himself if he wasn't working constantly."

Over the years, Palmer's fortunes have been inextricably linked to those of Mark McCormack. Although their original handshake was based on the understanding that he would represent only Arnold where sports marketing was concerned, McCormack represented Jack Nicklaus and Gary Player in the 1960s with Palmer's blessing. In 1970, Nicklaus broke away to manage his own affairs. But by then, McCormack had begun to build an empire of his own. International Management Group currently employs 1,500 people in 19 countries and generates annual revenues in excess of $700,000,000. It specializes in athlete representation, television and film production, event management, and other sports marketing endeavors. And its clients include 80 "Fortune 500" corporations, the Winter Olympics, Wimbledon, and depending on how one calculates income, half of the 24 highest-grossing athletes in the world.

Palmer is IMG's flagship client, but the companies that comprise Arnold's business empire are separate entities from IMG. Arnold Palmer Enterprises is a holding company that serves as the hub of his corporate network. It receives all revenue derived from the commercial exploitation of Palmer's name, image, and services, such as product endorsements, licensing fees, appearance fees, book and video projects, and any income generated by the self-standing companies that constitute the rest of Palmer's domain. Those companies include the Palmer Course Design Company, which designs golf courses around the world; the Arnold Palmer Golf Management Company, which manages golf courses and recently introduced an Arnold Palmer Golf Academy, where people can learn to play the game "Arnie style"; Priester Aviation, which charters and services private planes; and automobile dealerships in Pennsylvania, South Carolina, North Carolina, Kentucky and California. Palmer also has significant shareholdings in ProGroup (a public company that manufactures Arnold Palmer golf equipment) and a nascent cable-TV golf channel. And of course, there's his financial interest in Bay Hill and the Latrobe Country Club.

Palmer himself is president of Arnold Palmer Enterprises. Alastair Johnston is its chief operating officer, and IMG provides various support services to avoid the need Palmer would have to retain a

> "*When I started on the tour, we were playing so that maybe we could be the head pro at a club. Now, thanks to Arnie and Mark McCormack, the guys on the tour are playing to buy the club.*"
>
> CHI CHI RODRIGUEZ

worldwide staff if his companies were doing everything on their own. But Arnold is not just a figurehead executive. He takes his business responsibilities very seriously. Johnston might be the point man for Arnold Palmer Enterprises, but he never makes a major move without first discussing it with Palmer. And Arnold understands how to use his name and reputation to maximum advantage. There's a natural executive quality about him. He's conservative when it comes to business decisions. And while he might not be a genius at deal-making, he's smart enough to rely on people who are.

The Palmer Course Design Company typifies Palmer's corporate empire. Headquartered in Ponte Vedra Beach, Florida, it was founded in 1979, and has designed approximately 150 courses in 32 countries. The company charges $1 million plus travel expenses for each job. It doesn't actually build golf courses. For its million dollars, PCDC creates a master land-use plan; prepares blueprints, detail drawings, and other specifications; assists its clients in negotiating with contractors; and monitors construction. Palmer personally visits each site four or five times during the course of a job, signs off on final blueprints, and offers suggestions on

Palmer with Alastair Johnston, the Chief Operating Officer of Arnold Palmer Enterprises. In addition to fulfilling his corporate responsibilities, Johnston is a golf historian who has accumulated one of the largest collections of golf books in the world.

everything from the location of ponds to smaller details like the selection and placement of specific trees. And then he plays the course at its grand opening – no small matter, since for overseas tournaments he generally receives an appearance fee of $100,000 to $150,000.

The Palmer Course Design Company has built its share of courses that are unforgettable because of one spectacular quality or another. But perhaps more important to its philosophy is Palmer's focus on his clients' bottom line. "All of us have heard horror stories about signature designers," says Ed Seay, PCDC's executive vice president. "Some of them come in at the last minute, take one look after the irrigation system is in the ground, and tell the contractor to 'move that hill' after the hill has already been moved twice. But that's not Arnold's style. He might come in and say, 'Ed, this doesn't look right. Why don't we add a bunker here, or slide that green out a little, or move the tees back a bit.' But then he'll ask, 'If we do it, what will it cost the client?'"

"We have three goals in designing a course," Seay continues. "We want it to be beautiful; we want it to be challenging; and we want it to be fun. Our work is traditional, because that's the way

Arnold wants it. We never got into that trend of the '80s, building wild, difficult courses. Occasionally, a client comes to us and says, 'I want the toughest course ever built' or 'the widest fairways' or 'the smallest greens.' But most of the time, that's not what we hear. And we try to give people a course where good shots are rewarded and bad shots are punished; a course that doesn't require all the gold in Fort Knox to build or all the diamonds in South Africa to operate."

A typical Arnold Palmer golf course costs $3 to $5 million dollars for construction, plus the cost of land, clubhouse facilities, and Palmer's fee. "We think we're worth the million dollars," Seay says in closing. "We do a good job, and the public has a certain perception of what it means for a golf course to have Arnold's signature on it.

Arnold's involvement reflects positively on the entire development. People who invest in the project at the beginning, buy a home nearby, or join a club when the course opens feel that they're associating with a winner. So, sure, sometimes people say to me, 'You guys are charging a million dollars, and this other guy will do the job for two hundred thousand. Are you worth the difference?' And I tell them, 'Maybe not; but I do know that we'll spend your money wisely; and the one thing you can't get for $200,000 is Arnold Palmer.'"

Not everything Palmer touches turns to gold. At one point, he was president and a minority partner of the Isleworth Club in Windermere, Florida. The club was surrounded by several lakes, one of which flooded; and some nearby residents sued, claiming that the construction and maintenance of Isleworth's golf course had polluted the lake and caused the flooding. Palmer was found to have no personal liability, but the plaintiffs won the early stages of the litigation, and Isleworth was ultimately forced into bankruptcy.

Still, for the most part, the Palmer name is golden. His "Q Score," as it's known in the advertising industry, ranks consistently in the top-five among sports figures when the public is asked, "Do you know him; do you like him; do you trust him?" At present, he has endorsement contracts with Cadillac, Pennzoil, Textron, PaineWebber, GTE, Rayovac, Rolex, Lanier, and several dozen other companies. And while the terms of these affiliations vary, all are lucrative. For example, in 1988, Hertz paid Palmer $400,000 to serve as a company spokesman. But of equal note, that same year, Hertz bought 60,000 cars from Palmer automobile dealerships. Pennzoil has paid Arnold a flat annual fee for personal appearances and commercials for 15 years. And Palmer takes his role as a spokesperson seriously;

Three of approximately 150 courses designed worldwide by The Palmer Course Design Company.
Top: PGA West, La Quinta, California; center: Kapalua Resort, Hawaii;
bottom: Barton Creek Golf Course, Austin, Texas.

so much so that Winnie states, "It always bothers Arnie when a contract is over and he changes from, say, Lincoln to Cadillac. He can't quite get over the fact that he's been telling everyone how wonderful a certain product is, and now he's saying the same thing about a competitor. He really prefers to stay with the same company. I know if Quaker State offered Arnie twice the money he's getting from Pennzoil, I'd be very surprised if he switched. It's really true, what he says in that commercial, about riding on his father's lap on the tractor when he was a boy. And his father always did use Pennzoil."

One of the most interesting things about Palmer's success is that, despite widespread resentment toward athletes' salaries today, very few people begrudge Arnold his wealth. Rather, the public seems to feel that his financial position is

A Palmer foursome: brother Jerry, and sisters Lois Jean Tilley and Sandy Sarni, with Arnold at the Latrobe Country Club.

the logical extension of his personality and accomplishments. In the words of the *Washington Post*'s Shirley Povich, "Arnold Palmer is probably the world's most unresented millionaire." And sportswriter Frank Deford adds, "I don't think people know, or for that matter really care, what Arnold is like as a person. They think he's a nice guy; that certainly comes across. But beyond that, his image is a product of style and what he's done on the golf course rather than the substance of his personality."

But there's a great deal of substance to Palmer's personality. He's a man with definite views and values, and he's not afraid to speak his mind. Palmer's values were formed in a small Pennsylvania town. He went to college in the South. And the consensus of people who know him well is that he's changed very little over the years. Bob Drum, who met Palmer at an amateur tournament when Arnold was 16, says, "Outside of the fact that he's gotten a little hard of hearing lately, you could write the same things about him now that I wrote 48 years ago." Ray Cave, whose friendship with Palmer dates to 1960, recalls, "When I first met Arnold, he was a conservative guy out of a conservative background, and he's changed very little since then." And Winnie Palmer voices the view, "Arnie has never forgotten his roots or changed from the person he once was. He's gotten smarter as he's gone along; I guess we all do. But he's never gotten too full of himself, and he's always kept his feet on the ground. That's what's been so neat about it all."

Even today, Palmer retains the wonder of a boy when discussing the heroes of his youth. "If I could go back in time and meet people I've never met," he says, "I'd like to meet the Wright brothers, Charles Lindbergh, and Will Rogers. And going back further, I'd like to know if there really was a Robin Hood in Sherwood Forest, and if there was, what he was like." Palmer's values are the ones he was taught during childhood. "Family, loyalty, and hard work are everything to my father," says his daughter Peg. "Where family is concerned, he knows how he thinks things should be, and that's the end of it. His work ethic speaks for itself. And as for loyalty, he gives it and he expects it, absolute and complete."

But more than anything else, Palmer believes in "the American dream," and feels a vested interest in preserving the system that has allowed him to succeed. "My heroes are traditional American people," he proclaims. "Dwight Eisenhower, John Wayne, Bob Hope. All Dwight Eisenhower ever wanted was to make America the ideal place to be. And as far as I'm concerned, it is. One of the wonderful things about this country is, you don't have to do anything you don't want to do."

Over the years, Palmer has come to be regarded as an American icon. Norman Rockwell painted his portrait. Commentators liken his appeal to that of Johnny Carson. He's one of those people, like Bob Hope and Billy Graham, who presidents of the United States find it pleasant and politically advantageous to associate with. Yet his Americanism hasn't left him without critics. "There's a world out there that Arnold Palmer

Norman Rockwell acknowledged Palmer's status as an American icon with this 1972 portrait.

doesn't seem to understand," Arthur Ashe said shortly before he died. "Everything I know about Arnold leads me to believe that he's a decent man. And obviously, he appreciates the opportunities that this country has given him. But he doesn't seem to realize that there are a lot of children in America today who don't have the opportunities he had as a boy. Many of them are no better off than children growing up under totalitarian governments in the third world today. Life is harder and more complicated for them than Arnold makes it out to be, and I'm not sure how often or how deeply he thinks about those things. Most people don't. But when I see someone with his influence and great gifts not use that influence and gifts for the broadest good possible, it saddens me."

Part of the response to Ashe's comments lies in the fact that Palmer has long been involved in a number of charitable ventures. For 20 years, he served as National Chairman of the March of Dimes Birth Defects Foundation. He's also played a major fund-raising role for the Arnold Palmer Hospital for Children and Women in Orlando. And as a member of the Latrobe Area Hospital board of directors, he hosts an annual golf gala that last year raised $500,000. "Arnie's mind is so set on golf and other interests," Winnie Palmer explains, "that he's inclined not to look outside his own world unless someone comes to him and says 'please do this' or 'you really should come to the hospital.' But once he's aware of a problem and gets involved, he gives generously of his time and finds the experience rewarding."

Also, from a political standpoint, Palmer has a set of values that differs in many respects from those of Ashe and others who have suggested that he speak out on America's problems with a more activist view. Palmer's political beliefs are important to him. They're consistent with his understanding of what it means to be an American, and he's politically conservative. "My father was a Democrat," Arnold acknowledges. "He thought Roosevelt hung the moon, but I'm the opposite. I think you solve problems through family and personal charity. The less that big government and big-name outsiders get involved, the better it is for us all." Thus, Palmer opposes the expansion of most government entitlement programs, and reflects favorably on the Reagan-Bush era. He's currently at loggerheads with his alma mater, Wake Forest, over a university course on homosexual writers. And of politics in general, he says, "I have strong opinions, but I've made a conscious decision not to make a big issue of them

Palmer served as National Chairman of the March of Dimes Birth Defects Foundation for 20 years, raising money for children like Carmen Donesa, National Poster Child, 1971.

publicly. I voice my opinions to my friends and family, generally in a conservative way. There are times when I'm tempted to be more outspoken; but usually I think about it for a day or two and pull in because I don't want to be like a lot of people who I hear voicing opinions publicly. So when I'm outraged about something, politically or whatever, I express myself in the office and at home. Then I hear from the people who've heard me; and it's rare that I get a hundred percent agreement on what I've said, so I drop it."

With regard to racial issues that have surfaced on the PGA Tour, Palmer also takes a conservative view. When the PGA was founded in 1916, its charter had a "Caucasians only" clause. That remained in effect until 1961; and it wasn't until 1969 that a black man, Charlie Sifford, won on the PGA Tour. Meanwhile, the Masters continued to require an "invitation" for entry; and in 1973, Sifford was moved to say, "The Masters is the last stronghold of bias. It's a lily-white club, and the white people seem to want it that way." Two years later, that tradition was broken, when Lee Elder was invited to play at Augusta by virtue of his victory in the 1974 Monsanto Open. But even today, the Augusta National Golf Club has no women and only one black member. Surveying the PGA as a whole, the touring pros are overwhelmingly white; the club pros are overwhelmingly white; and the vast majority of spectators at golf tournaments are white.

The issue came to a head in 1990 when the Shoal Creek Country Club in Birmingham, Alabama, was scheduled to host the PGA Championship. Shoal Creek had no black members; and its president declared in an interview that none would be admitted in the future, although blacks who qualified would be allowed to play in the PGA. That led to a firestorm of protest against the fact that a club with an openly discriminatory membership policy was hosting a "major" tournament. And several sponsors of ABC's event coverage threatened to withdraw $2,000,000 worth of advertising if Shoal Creek didn't admit a black member. Then, nine days before the tournament began, the club extended an "honorary membership" to a local black businessman, enabling the PGA Championship to proceed as planned.

Palmer's opinion on the Shoal Creek controversy was in keeping with the rest of his philosophy. "I'm a firm believer in the right of a private club to be private," he says. "And I think the members of that club should be able to accept and reject new members as they see fit. However, at the same time, I believe that, if you have a public event at your club, you have an obligation to follow the rules of society. I've always advocated that anyone with the ability to play should be allowed to play in any tournament. Now, you might say that holding the PGA at Shoal Creek somehow validates that club's membership policy. But other than public golf courses, there isn't a club in America that doesn't have restrictions, whether those restrictions are based on race, color, creed, or whatever. And if you allow one restriction, where do you draw the line? So where I come out on the issue is, as long as a tournament admits everyone who's eligible to play and abides by the rules of society, I have no problem with it being held at Shoal Creek or anyplace else."

Palmer's views have not gone without response. "Outside of those Hertz commercials he made with O.J. Simpson," asks one critic, "can anyone remember seeing Arnold Palmer with a black person?" And Jerry Izenberg adds, "I wish Arnold had done more to push integration at the Masters when he was winning all those tournaments. And certainly, he could do more to promote equality of opportunity and racial understanding today." Still, Palmer's beliefs are what they are. And among the people who speak well of him on the issue of race is Charlie Sifford.

> *"You don't pal with Arnold Palmer; you don't hang out with Arnold Palmer. The only people who hang out with Palmer are his very good friends. But at the same time, he's not stand-offish with anybody. I don't think I've ever known an athlete who was more gracious with others."*
>
> LEROY NEIMAN

"I always said I'd never ask Arnold Palmer, Jack Nicklaus, Gary Player, none of those guys, to fight my battle," Sifford says. "Arnold Palmer was a powerful man at Augusta. But the man who ran that tournament, Clifford Roberts, was tough as nails. He made that statement once that, as long as he was alive, there wouldn't be nothing but white golfers and black caddies in the Masters. So it's hard to say what would have happened if Arnold had stepped up and said something about integrating the Masters. The first thing that would have happened is, some people would have called him a nigger lover. Then his income would have gone down. And after that, who knows? To be honest, I wouldn't have jeopardized myself for something like that, so I don't hold anything against Arnold. He and I always got along fine. I respected him, and he respected me. We used to get together for a couple of beers and have a good time. I never asked him for anything. If I had, I don't know if he would have said yes or turned me down. But to take the lead on a racial matter, that's not the way he was, and I didn't think that was his obligation. Some people might say that a person with as much power as Arnold had should have used it more. But Arnold wasn't the type of person to lead in that way. And I'll tell you

"It's not my job to change the world. I treat people the way I'd like to be treated. I try to be respectful and kind to everyone. I have my views on politics and other issues, but I've never tried to force my views on anyone else. Some people agree with me; some people don't. But in America, there's room for disagreement. We don't all have to have the same point of view."

ARNOLD PALMER

something. If everyone in this country treated everyone else the way Arnold treats people, a lot of the problems we have wouldn't be."

Given the appeal of Palmer's personality and the strength of his views, the possibility of his becoming a candidate for public office has been discussed many times. "I'm not clever enough," was Arnold's response when the issue was first raised in 1964. Five years later, political columnists Rowland Evans and Robert Novak reported, "Republican leaders are considering the possibility that golfing great Arnold Palmer of Latrobe, Pennsylvania, will become their candidate for governor in 1970." Once again, Palmer declined, telling the press, "I was approached informally to see what my interest would be, but the interest is not really there." However, this time he left the door ajar, adding, "I have no ambition to enter politics at this time." Then, in 1973, rumors that Palmer would seek the governorship were fueled by his own remarks. "I guess everyone has political thoughts," he said on a visit to the state capitol in Harrisburg. "I've thought about it because everybody keeps bringing it up. I've never really given it serious thought, but you never know. What we need is someone who is interested in the state and not in himself, someone who would look at the state without selfish thoughts."

Ultimately, Palmer decided not to take the plunge. "I've been asked to run for Governor five or six times," he said in June 1973. "But I'd have to stop playing golf competitively, and I'm not inclined toward that at this time. Someday though; sure, I'm interested." Meanwhile, looking back on it all, Winnie Palmer says, "I don't think Arnie ever seriously entertained the idea of running for Governor. At least, I hope not. He was flattered by it. And for a while, he had the misguided idea that he could get in there and maybe do something for his state and his country. That's a sacrifice he would have been willing to make; and for Arnie, it would have been a sacrifice. But I was very much against it, and always will be. Know-

Palmer was honored to address a joint session of Congress on the 100th anniversary of Dwight Eisenhower's birth.

ing Arnie as well as I do, I think being in politics would eat him up. I just don't think Arnie is made for politics."

Still, it's easy to imagine a Palmer campaign patterned on those of Ronald Reagan. The public has always seen what it wants to see in Arnold. On the one hand, he's a conservative multimillionaire tycoon who has supported 11 Republican candidates for president in a row. Yet, in the steel mills and coal mines of middle-America, he remains a working-class hero. That's a pretty good political base. And Dow Finsterwald, one of Arnold's closest friends over the decades, speaks to what makes Palmer such a reassuring figure when he says, "If I was in trouble and could have one person to turn to, it would be Arnold Palmer. If I was a soldier, I'd want Arnold to be my leader. And if I was in battle, I'd want as many soldiers like Arnold as I could have fighting beside me."

Nonetheless, the likelihood is that Palmer's place in history will come as a result of what he did on the golf course, not in politics or any other arena. And thus, the question arises: "How does he rank among the greats of golf?" Perhaps the first thing to note in that regard is, in virtually all sports, today's stars are better than yesterday's, and tomorrow's will be better than those of today. A lot of fans are reluctant to accept that; they worship the heroes of their youth. But all anyone has to do is look at an Olympic record book to see how few men's gold-medal winners from earlier Olympic competitions would even qualify for the finals in today's women's events. And golf is no different from other sports. The current players are stronger and drive the ball farther than their counterparts from the past. There are more of them, so the competition is fiercer. And because of new playing techniques, advanced training and changes in equipment, the game keeps improving. It used to be that, if a golfer wound up in a bunker – "Uh oh; here comes a bogey." Now players hit into bunkers all the time without losing a stroke to par.

Thus, golfers, like other athletes, have to be judged within their era. And Palmer was superb. "In my opinion," says Herbert Warren Wind, "Jack Nicklaus was the greatest golfer of all time. And after Jack, you have Bobby Jones, Ben Hogan, and Harry Vardon. But Arnold was magnificent. When I think of him, I think of a burst of sunlight. Not only did he have courage on the golf course; he played beautiful shots that none of us had ever seen before."

During the course of his career, Palmer won 61 victories on the U.S. tour, placing him fourth on the all-time list behind Snead, Nicklaus, and Hogan. His eight "major" titles (including the 1954 USGA Amateur Championship) are surpassed by only five other golfers. From 1957 through 1971, he was among the top-10 money winners on the PGA tour. He won at least one PGA tournament every year from 1955 through 1971 – a remarkable 17-season run. On four separate occasions, he captured the

In 1993, Palmer was honored as one of the five inaugural recipients of The National Sports Award. The other recipients were Kareem Abdul-Jabbar, Muhammad Ali, Wilma Rudolph and Ted Williams.

Vardon Trophy, awarded annually to the golfer with the lowest official-tournament scoring average. And in one five-year span, from 1960 through 1964, Palmer entered 19 "majors" and won six while finishing in the top-five 14 times and in the top-10 on 16 occasions.

"That's greatness," says Bob Costas, who observes, "In ranking athletes, you can't just go with lifetime numbers. Some athletes establish their immortality in a relatively short period of time. There are men in the Hall of Fame who've won twice as many games as Sandy Koufax, but Koufax had seasons that were as good as any pitcher ever. The way he pitched during the last four years of his career was almost beyond belief. It wasn't just the numbers he put up; it was the way he flat-out dominated. Watching Koufax, you knew in an instant that he was special. And that's the way Arnold was in his prime."

Only one other golfer since the Eisenhower era has matched Palmer's record of achievement; and that, of course, is Jack Nicklaus. Nicklaus was the tour's leading money-winner for eight seasons, and among its top-four for an astounding 17 consecutive years. As far as "majors" are concerned, only four men in history have won the Masters, the

"If I spend enough time with someone in a foursome on the golf course, I can tell you just about everything you want to know about him, from whether you can trust him to what kind of businessman he is to whether or not he's someone you want to be with at all."

ARNOLD PALMER

U.S. Open, the British Open, and the PGA during the course of their career. Ben Hogan, Gene Sarazen, and Gary Player won each title at least once. Nicklaus won each "major" three or more times. On five occasions, he won two majors in the same year – the first time in 1963, when he was 23 years old, and the last time in 1980, when he was 40. He won six Masters titles, including one at age 46; five PGA Championships; four U.S. Opens; three British Opens; and two USGA Amateur crowns. He's currently working on a string of 37 consecutive U.S. Open appearances. And out of 20 "majors" entered from 1971 through 1975, he won six, and finished in the top-five on 18 occasions and in the top-10 all 20 times. And while it's true that Nicklaus always had a 10-year age advantage over Palmer where their direct competition was concerned, Deane Beman, the current PGA Tour commissioner, put that edge aside when he said simply, "Lay the records out from the time Jack turned pro until now, and it's plain as day. The man buried Palmer."

Still, despite his extraordinary achievements, there are ways in which Jack has been unable to equal Arnold. Nicklaus's immortality is based on winning, whereas Palmer's is based on being Palmer. "A lot of great players come and go in sports," says Frank Deford, "but only a handful take their sport somewhere. Babe Ruth did it; Muhammad Ali did it. And so did Arnold Palmer. He made golf a major sport, and brought it to the masses. And in a way, that makes him more important than Jack, because Jack is merely the greatest golfer who ever lived. A hundred years from now, when their records speak for themselves, Nicklaus might be better known than Palmer. But that won't diminish Arnold's accomplishments. He's the guy who made it happen."

"Arnold's the one who made us cover golf," says Jerry Izenberg. "Because of him, a serious sportswriter couldn't miss the Masters or U.S. Open. And what was so appealing about him wasn't just that he was a great golfer, but that he was such a great competitor and an even better champion. He won't be remembered for the perfect game, the longest drives, the best iron-play, or whatever. But when someone uses the words 'golf' and 'hero' in the same sentence, people will think of Arnold Palmer."

"There are no major or minor sports," Palmer once said. "The way a man participates in a sport makes it major or minor." And following that creed, he has devoted himself to the finest traditions of his sport. "Arnold has always shown the highest respect for golf," says Gary Player. "In a very real sense, the game as a whole always meant more to him than how he personally did in a tournament. I've never heard him complain about a loss or bad luck or another person being lucky. He knows how to share a moment of triumph, whether it's his or someone else's. And nobody loves golf more than Arnold. Look at what he's done for the sport. The American press was inclined to forget that golf was played in other parts of the world. And by going to St. Andrews, Arnold almost single-handedly returned the British Open to its rightful position of grandeur. He's our foremost ambassador to the world, and the international symbol of excellence in golf."

"Golf is fortunate that the person who came along with the advent of television was Arnold Palmer," says Dow Finsterwald, putting things further in perspective. "Someone else could have won just as many tournaments and not done half as much for the game as Arnold. Not only did he have all the personal qualities you look for in a champion, he was totally committed to everything that's good about golf."

"I won the PGA at Laurel Valley in 1965," adds Dave Marr. "It was my first major; my biggest win ever. And I'll never forget, after the press conference, Arnold invited me over to his house, sat me down, and talked to me in a very nice caring way for at least two hours about what I could expect now that I'd been elevated to a higher status and what my new responsibilities were. His place in history will probably be as much as a personality as a player. As a person, he's been an inspiration to everyone who plays the game. He gave us an image and a sense of honor that, to my knowledge, no other athlete ever bestowed upon his sport. And it's funny. So much attention has been paid to Arnold's personal qualities that I really don't think he gets enough credit for how good a golfer he was. Only three men in history won more tournaments. Arnold was one of the greatest drivers who ever played. And when he was young, he was the best long putter I ever saw."

Palmer hasn't triumphed in a "major" since 1964. And he hasn't won a regular PGA tournament in 21 years. Nonetheless, he continues to play, aging gracefully with every stroke. Lee Trevino speaks for his brethren when he says, "Arnold is the greatest role model that any sport ever had. When a young fellow comes on the tour today, sooner or later one of the old-timers like myself will take him aside and say, 'Study that man. Look at the way he loves the game, conducts himself, and treats other people. Arnold Palmer is the one you want to be like.'"

Meanwhile, Palmer says simply, "I'd like to be remembered as someone who made a serious contribution to the traditions and principles of golf. I can't really explain how much the game has meant to me. All I can say is that I'll never be able to give back an equal amount in return. If there's one thing I'm particularly proud of in my career, it's that, when I started, they said only rich people played the game. And I like to think I changed that, so that now everybody can play golf. Now if only I could play it a little better this year . . . "

"That's the one thing Arnie regrets," Winnie Palmer says in closing, "that he doesn't play as well as he used to. It bothers him.

"Arnold's place in history will be as the man who took golf from being a game for the few to a sport of the masses. He was the catalyst who made that happen."

JACK NICKLAUS

Sometimes he says to me, 'I'm getting old; I've lost distance; I don't have confidence in my putting anymore.' But Arnie is an optimist, and one of the great things about golf is that there's always another round. So he hopes it will all come back to him, even if just for a day. And if it comes back for a day, then why not four days? I know it would mean a lot to Arnie to win a tournament again, and I hope he never stops trying."

On April 8, 1993, a 63-year-old man with a warm smile and thinning hair stepped up to the first tee at the Augusta National Golf Club and hooked his drive into a cluster of trees. Then he played a textbook recovery shot, and sank a 10-foot putt to birdie the first hole of the 1993 Masters. On the par-5 second hole, he pitched his third shot to within six feet of the flag and followed with his second birdie in a row. And on the third hole, he rolled in a 15-foot birdie putt to go three under par.

Arnold Palmer was leading the Masters. And across Augusta, the word rippled through the crowd, spreading like wildfire through the azaleas and pines: "Arnie's got it going again. Arnie's on a roll."

"*Palmer fit beautifully with the 1960s. But unlike many other great athletes, he would have fit in and stood out in any era. I can easily imagine him in the Roaring Twenties with Babe Ruth, Jack Dempsey, and Red Grange. Or in the 1980s with Wayne Gretzky, Joe Montana, Larry Bird and Magic Johnson.*"

DICK SCHAAP

Thank you

"I'd like to express to the world the deep appreciation and gratitude I feel for the opportunity I've had during my lifetime to do the things I've wanted to do."

ARNOLD PALMER

America for

letting me do

my own thing.

"Manufacturers now understand the physics of club design and what happens when club meets ball. They're able to redistribute weight with different metals and compounds so that clubs maintain their structural integrity and balance, and at the same time, have a larger sweet spot than before. A golfer today can mishit a ball by a fraction of an inch, and it will stay on the fairway and go almost as far as if it had been hit perfectly. Thirty years ago, the same shot might have been short and in the rough."

ARNOLD PALMER

Palmer's private collection of approximately 10,000 clubs is among the largest in the world.

The current tools of Palmer's trade.

Top left to bottom right: The celebrity of it all. Palmer with ... Ed Sullivan in 1960;
Jackie Gleason, as part of a two-hour CBS Special; Michael Jordan, Ameritech Pro-Am, Chicago, 1993;
Dwight Eisenhower, early 1960s; Jimmy Durante, Hollywood, California, 1947; George Bush, 1986;
Bob Hope and Dean Martin, receiving 1960 Golfer-of-the-Year Trophy; Joe Louis, at a Pro-Am in L.A.

"General Eisenhower was certainly a better player than the average American who played golf. He hit the ball pretty well, but the strongest part of his game was his desire. Richard Nixon wasn't really a golfer. Gerald Ford had an 18 handicap and deserved every bit of it, but he hit the ball hard. Ford's problem was, he had the yips putting. George Bush plays to a 14 handicap, and now that he has more free time, I think his game will get better. Bill Clinton has the potential to be a very good golfer. He putts the ball very well. He's strong and has a keen interest in the game. His swing is pretty good, and he has a lot of determination to be a good player."

ARNOLD PALMER

"Of all the perks of office, the one I've enjoyed most
is playing 18 holes of golf with Arnold Palmer."

BILL CLINTON

"Here's a man who's 64 years old. He's still open to new business ideas.
He still travels all over the world. He still plays golf every day he can.
His energy level is extraordinary."

DOC GIFFIN

Above: Four of Arnold and Winnie's grandchildren, left to right: Anne, Katherine, Sam, Emily.
Below left: Arnold with business associate and longtime family friend, Doc Giffin.
Below right: Arnold and Winnie. Facing page: Arnold, with Riley, faithful companion of 13 years.

"*Arnold Palmer epitomizes the American dream. You look at him and say to yourself, 'This is what success is all about. People adore him; he's the best in the world at what he does; he loves life; he's got a great family; his peers respect him.' Arnold Palmer is more than someone to look up to. He's someone you can dream about.*"

PAT SUMMERALL

"If I die tomorrow, well, I'm playing golf. That's the way it's supposed to be. My father played 27 holes the day he passed away, and enjoyed every bit of it. Not the passing away, of course."

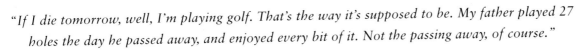

ARNOLD PALMER

"I can't tell you how much I appreciate what the game has done for me. I look at the people I've met and the associations I've made through golf. I met my wife, Winnie, through golf. I can't give enough to golf. If I had more, I'd give more. Everything I have I owe to golf. When you honor me, that's a falsehood; you're honoring golf."

ARNOLD PALMER

USGA AMATEUR CHAMPIONSHIP TOURNAMENTS

1948

Memphis Country Club,
Memphis, Tennessee
*Lost in first round to William K.
Barrett Jr., Colonial CC,
Memphis, Tennessee, 6 and 5*

1949

Oak Hill Country Club,
Rochester, New York
*Lost in third round to Crawford
Rainwater, Pensacola, Florida,
4 and 3, after defeating Frederick
Mayer, Westchester, N.Y., 3 and 2,
and Charles Robinson, Belle
Meade, Tennessee, 4 and 3*

1950

Minneapolis Country Club,
Minneapolis, Minnesota
*Lost in first round to Frank
Stranahan, Toledo, Ohio, 4 and 3*

1951

Did not compete, serving in
Coast Guard

1952

Did not compete, serving in
Coast Guard

1953

Oklahoma City Golf and
Country Club, Oklahoma
City, Oklahoma
*Lost in fourth round to Don
Albert, Alliance, Ohio, 1 up,
after defeating John Frazier,
Finlay, N.C., 7 and 5; Jack
Westland, Everett, Washington,
1 up, and Ken Venturi, San
Francisco, 2 and 1. (Shot 78 in
losing match to Albert)*

1954

Detroit Golf Club,
Detroit, Michigan
*Won championship with follow-
ing sequence of victories:
Defeated Frank Strafaci, Garden
City, N.Y., 1 up. Defeated John
Veghte, Pine Brook, N.Y., 1 up.
Defeated Richard Whiting, Red
Run, Michigan, 2 and 1. Defeated
Walter Andzel, South Shore,
N.Y., 5 and 3. Defeated Frank
Stranahan, Toledo, Ohio, 3 and
1. Defeated Don Cherry, Wichita
Falls, Texas, 1 up. Defeated Ed
Meister, Kirtland, Ohio, 1 up,
39 holes. Defeated Bob Sweeny,
Sands Point, N.Y., 1 up*

OTHER AMATEUR HIGHLIGHTS

1946

Winner, WPIAL and PIAA
Championships
Runnerup, Hearst Junior

1947

Winner, WPIAL and PIAA
Championships
Winner, West Penn Junior
(df C.A. Brown, 5 and 4, at
Highland CC)
Winner, West Penn Amateur
(df Knox Young, 3 and 2,
at Shannopin CC)
Semifinalist, Pennsylvania
Amateur

1948

Winner, Southern Conference
Championship
Semifinalist, North and South
Amateur
Lost, first round, U.S. Amateur

1949

Winner, Southern Conference
Championship
Winner, West Penn Amateur
(df Jack Benson at Oakmont)
Semifinalist, North and
South Amateur
Medalist, National
Intercollegiate (NCAA)
Lost, third round, U.S. Amateur

1950

Winner, Southern Intercollegiate
Winner, West Penn Amateur
(df Steve Savor at Longue Vue)
Medalist, National
Intercollegiate (NCAA)
Lost, first round, U.S. Amateur

1951

Winner, West Penn Amateur
(df Jack Mahaffey at Alcoma)
Winner, Worsham Memorial

1952

Winner, West Penn Amateur
(df Frank Souchak at Fox Chapel)
Runnerup, Pennsylvania
Amateur (playoff)

1953

Winner, Ohio Amateur
Winner, Cleveland Amateur
Semifinalist, West Penn
Amateur
Winner, Mayfield Heights Open
Lost, fourth round,
U.S. Amateur
Missed cut, U.S. Open

1954

Winner, Ohio Amateur
Winner, All-American Amateur
Winner, Atlantic Coast
Conference Championship
Winner, Bill Waite
Memorial Tournament
Runnerup, World Amateur
Missed cut, U.S. Open

As a young man, Palmer was already regarded
by the local press as a hero.

1955

Canadian Open [1]

1956

Panama Open
Colombia Open
Insurance City Open [1]
Eastern Open [1]

1957

Houston Open [1]
Azalea Open [1]
Rubber City Open [1]
San Diego Open [1]

1958

St. Petersburg Open [1]
Masters Tournament [1]
Pepsi Open [1]

1959

Thunderbird Invitational [1]
Oklahoma City Open [1]
West Palm Beach Open [1]

1960

Bob Hope Desert Classic [1]
Texas Open [1]
Baton Rouge Open [1]
Pensacola Open [1]
Masters Tournament [1]
U.S. Open Championship [1]
Insurance City Open [1]
Mobile Open [1]
Canada Cup
  (Partner: Sam Snead)

1961

San Diego Open [1]
Phoenix Open [1]
Baton Rouge Open [1]
Texas Open [1]
British Open Championship
Western Open [1]

1962

Bob Hope Desert Classic [1]
Phoenix Open [1]
Masters Tournament [1]
Texas Open [1]
Tournament of Champions [1]
Colonial National Invitational [1]
British Open Championship
American Golf Classic [1]
Canada Cup
  (Partner: Sam Snead)

1963

Los Angeles Open [1]
Phoenix Open [1]
Pensacola Open [1]
Thunderbird Classic [1]
Cleveland Open [1]
Western Open [1]
Whitemarsh Open [1]
Australian Wills Masters
Canada Cup
  (Partner: Jack Nicklaus)

1964

Masters Tournament [1]
Oklahoma City Open [1]
Piccadilly World Match Play
  Championship
Canada Cup
  (Partner: Jack Nicklaus)

1965

Tournament of Champions [1]

1966

Los Angeles Open [1]
Tournament of Champions [1]
Australian Open
Houston Champions
  International [1]
PGA Team Championship [1]
  (Partner: Jack Nicklaus)
Canada Cup
  (Partner: Jack Nicklaus)

1967

Los Angeles Open [1]
Tucson Open [1]
American Golf Classic [1]
Thunderbird Classic [1]
Piccadilly World Match Play
  Championship
  (Partner: Jack Nicklaus)
World Cup
  (Partner: Jack Nicklaus)
World Cup International
  Trophy (Individual Title)

1968

Bob Hope Desert Classic [1]
Kemper Open [1]

1969

Heritage Classic [1]
Danny Thomas-Diplomat
  Classic [1]

1970

PGA Team Championship [1]
  (Partner: Jack Nicklaus)

1971

Bob Hope Desert Classic [1]
Citrus Open [1]
Westchester Classic [1]
PGA Team Championship [1]
  (Partner: Jack Nicklaus)
Lancôme Trophy

1973

Bob Hope Desert Classic [1]

1975

Spanish Open
British PGA Championship

1980

Canadian PGA Championship
PGA Seniors Championship [2]

1981

USGA Senior Open
  Championship [2]

1982

Marlboro Senior Classic [2]
Denver Post Champions
  of Golf [2]

1983

Boca Grove Senior Classic [2]

1984

PGA Seniors Championship [2]
Doug Sanders Celebrity
  Pro-Am [2]
Senior TPC [2]
Quadel (Boca Grove) Classic [2]

1985

Senior TPC [2]

1986

Unionmutual Classic [2]

1988

Crestar Classic [2]

TOTAL VICTORIES: 92

[1] PGA Tour (61)
[2] Senior Events (12)

Palmer's 1960 Masters triumph brought him to center stage,
congratulated here by Bobby Jones as Winnie and Clifford Roberts look on.

1955

Total U.S. Tour Earnings	$	8,226
Total Foreign/International Earnings	$	900
Number of U.S. Tour Starts		31
Scoring Average		70.99

1956

Total U.S. Tour Earnings	$	20,044
Total Foreign/International Earnings	$	3,800
Number of U.S. Tour Starts		30
Scoring Average		71.14

1957

Total U.S. Tour Earnings	$	31,704
Number of U.S. Tour Starts		33
Scoring Average		71.09

1958

Total U.S. Tour Earnings	$	45,608
Total Foreign/International Earnings	$	613
Number of U.S. Starts		32
Scoring Average		70.66

1959

Total U.S. Tour Earnings	$	38,675
Number of U.S. Tour Starts		31
Scoring Average		70.51

1960

Total U.S. Tour Earnings	$	80,968
Total Foreign/International Earnings	$	3,870
Number of U.S. Tour Starts		27
Scoring Average		69.95

1961

Total U.S. Tour Earnings	$	65,002
Total Foreign/International Earnings	$	4,520
Number of U.S. Tour Starts		26
Scoring Average		69.78

1962

Total U.S. Tour Earnings	$	82,456
Total Foreign/International Earnings	$	5,820
Number of U.S. Tour Starts		21
Scoring Average		70.27

1963

Total U.S. Tour Earnings	$	130,835
Total Foreign/International Earnings	$	3,240
Number of U.S. Tour Starts		20
Scoring Average		70.63

1964

Total U.S. Tour Earnings	$	116,089
Total Foreign/International Earnings	$	16,003
Number of U.S. Tour Starts		26
Scoring Average		70.24

1965

Total U.S. Tour Earnings	$	82,700
Total Foreign/International Earnings	$	5,600
Number of U.S. Tour Starts		22
Scoring Average		71.42

1966

Total U.S. Tour Earnings	$	154,692
Total Foreign/International Earnings	$	10,436
Number of U.S. Tour Starts		22
Scoring Average		70.69

1967

Total U.S. Tour Earnings	$	193,964
Total Foreign/International Earnings	$	16,000
Number of U.S. Tour Starts		25
Scoring Average		70.19

1968

Total U.S. Tour Earnings	$	114,603
Total Foreign/International Earnings	$	7,104
Number of U.S. Tour Starts		24
Scoring Average		70.94

1969

Total U.S. Tour Earnings	$	105,128
Number of U.S. Tour Starts		26
Scoring Average		70.99

1970

Total U.S. Tour Earnings	$	128,853
Total Foreign/International Earnings	$	7,358
Number of U.S. Tour Starts		22
Scoring Average		70.89

1971

Total U.S. Tour Earnings		$209,604
Total Foreign/International Earnings	$	24,216
Number of U.S. Tour Starts		24
Scoring Average		70.56

1972

Total U.S. Tour Earnings	$	84,181
Total Foreign/International Earnings	$	12,209
Number of U.S. Tour Starts		22
Scoring Average		71.41

1973

Total U.S. Tour Earnings	$	89,457
Total Foreign/International Earnings	$	12,180
Number of U.S. Tour Starts		22
Scoring Average		71.30

1974

Total U.S. Tour Earnings	$	36,293
Total Foreign/International Earnings	$	6,254
Number of U.S. Tour Starts		20
Scoring Average		72.45

1975

Total U.S. Tour Earnings	$	60,239
Total Foreign/International Earnings	$	36,334
Number of U.S. Tour Starts		20
Scoring Average		71.77

1976

Total U.S. Tour Earnings	$	21,186
Total Foreign/International Earnings	$	22,565
Number of U.S. Tour Starts		19
Scoring Average		72.05

1977

Total U.S. Tour Earnings	$	31,564
Total Foreign/International Earnings	$	9,368
Number of U.S. Tour Starts		22
Scoring Average		72.49

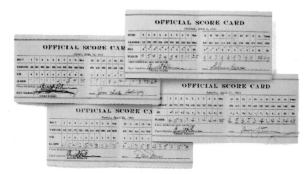

Palmer's scorecards from the 1964 Masters –
his fourth victory at Augusta and his final "major" win.

1978

Total U.S. Tour Earnings	$ 28,835
Total Foreign/International Earnings	$ 15,948
Number of U.S. Tour Starts	15
Scoring Average	72.87

1979

Total U.S. Tour Earnings	$ 12,043
Total Foreign/International Earnings	$ 8,348
Total U.S. Tour Starts	16
Scoring Average	73.69

1980

Total U.S. Tour Earnings	$ 19,637
Total Foreign/International Earnings	$ 27,619
Total Senior Tour Earnings	$ 54,000
Number of U.S. Tour Starts	14
Scoring Average	73.06
Number of Senior Tour Starts	3
Scoring Average	71.71

1981

Total U.S. Tour Earnings	$ 6,827
Total Foreign/International Earnings	$ 2,629
Total Senior Tour Earnings	$ 88,100
Number of U.S. Tour Starts	13
Scoring Average	73.83
Number of Senior Tour Starts	7
Scoring Average	71.39

1982

Total U.S. Tour Earnings	$ 9,327
Total Foreign/International Earnings	$ 11,549
Total Senior Tour Earnings	$ 109,818
Number of U.S. Tour Starts	11
Scoring Average	74.22
Number of Senior Tour Starts	10
Scoring Average	71.58

1983

Total U.S. Tour Earnings	$ 20,414
Total Foreign/International Earnings	$ 16,166
Total Senior Tour Earnings	$ 123,052
Total Non-Tour Seniors Earnings	$ 5,750
Number of U.S. Tour Starts	11
Scoring Average	73.84
Number of Senior Tour Starts	12
Scoring Average	70.93

1984

Total U.S. Tour Earnings	$ 4,952
Total Foreign/International Earnings	$ 443
Total Senior Tour Earnings	$ 218,065
Total Non-Tour Seniors Earnings	$ 5,750
Number of U.S. Tour Starts	8
Scoring Average	74.47
Number of Senior Tour Starts	15
Scoring Average	71.60

1985

Total U.S. Tour Earnings	$ 5,727
Total Senior Tour Earnings	$ 155,924
Number of U.S. Tour Starts	6
Scoring Average	74.17
Number of Senior Tour Starts	15
Scoring Average	71.45

1986

Total U.S. Tour Earnings	$ 4,200
Total Foreign/International Earnings	$ 2,900
Total Senior Tour Earnings	$ 218,331
Number of U.S. Tour Starts	6
Scoring Average	75.09
Number of Senior Tour Starts	17
Scoring Average	71.69

1987

Total U.S. Tour Earnings	$ 5,587
Total Foreign/International Earnings	$ 640
Total Senior Tour Earnings	$ 238,637
Total Non-Tour Seniors Earnings	$ 27,940
Number of U.S. Tour Starts	4
Scoring Average	76.08
Number of Senior Tour Starts	20
Scoring Average	71.79

1988

Total U.S. Tour Earnings	$ 3,120
Total Foreign/International Earnings	$ 34,616
Total Senior Tour Earnings	$ 274,499
Number of U.S. Tour Starts	5
Scoring Average	73.55
Number of Senior Tour Starts	18
Scoring Average	71.78

1989

Total U.S. Tour Earnings	$ 35,648
Total Foreign/International Earnings	$ 20,155
Total Senior Tour Earnings	$ 183,453
Total Non-Tour (U.S.) Earnings	$ 35,000
Number of U.S. Tour Starts	4
Scoring Average	76.00
Number of Senior Tour Starts	18
Scoring Average	72.26

1990

Total U.S. Tour Earnings	$ 73,000
Total Foreign/International Earnings	$ 14,615
Total Senior Tour Earnings	$ 117,011
Total Non-Tour (U.S.) Earnings	$ 25,500
Number of U.S. Tour Starts	4
Scoring Average	75.20
Number of Senior Tour Starts	18
Scoring Average	72.85

1991

Total U.S. Tour Earnings	$ 44,725
Total Senior Tour Earnings	$ 165,088
Total Non-Tour (U.S.) Earnings	$ 26,800
Total Non-Tour Senior Earnings	$ 9,641
Number of U.S. Tour Starts	5
Scoring Average	74.5
Number of Senior Tour Starts	18
Scoring Average	71.86

1992

Total U.S. Tour Earnings	$ 3,200
Total Senior Tour Earnings	$ 72,186
Total Non-Tour (U.S.) Earnings	$ 68,000
Total Non-Tour Senior Earnings	$ 13,588
Number of U.S. Tour Starts	5
Scoring Average	74.38
Number of Senior Tour Starts	20
Scoring Average	72.43

1993

Total U.S. Tour Earnings	$ 1,970
Total Senior Tour Earnings	$ 116,673
Total Non-Tour (U.S.) Earnings	$ 55,000
Total Non-Tour Seniors Earnings	$ 15,614
Number of U.S. Tour Starts	5
Scoring Average	75.36
Number of Senior Tour Starts	21
Scoring Average	72.94

*Total tour earnings shown may include
some unofficial events.*

For Palmer, the adulation and
demands of fame most likely will never end.

U.S. EARNINGS

Regular PGA Tour	$	2,090,039
Senior PGA Tour	$	1,924,022

FOREIGN/INTERNATIONAL/NON-TOUR U.S. EARNINGS

$ 707,375

TOTAL COMPETITIVE EARNINGS
(*Excludes pro-ams, skins games*)

$ 4,721,436

VICTORIES: 92

U.S. Tour – 61
Foreign/International – 19
Seniors – 12

INDIVIDUAL RECORDS

BEST 18-HOLE ROUND: 62

1959 Thunderbird Invitational, fourth round
1966 Los Angeles Open, third round

BEST OPENING ROUND: 64

1955 Canadian Open
1962 Phoenix Open
1970 Citrus Open
1970 Greensboro Open
1971 Westchester Classic

BEST SECOND ROUND: 63

1961 Texas Open

BEST THIRD ROUND: 62

1966 Los Angeles Open

BEST FOURTH ROUND: 62

1959 Thunderbird Classic

LOWEST SCORE, FIRST 36 HOLES: 130

1961 Texas Open (67-63)

LOWEST SCORE, FIRST 54 HOLES: 195

1955 Canadian Open (64-67-64)

LOWEST 72-HOLE SCORE: 265

1955 Canadian Open (64-67-64-70)

BIGGEST VICTORY MARGIN: 12

1962 Phoenix Open

MOST CONSECUTIVE BIRDIES: 7

1966 Los Angeles Open, third round

HOLES-IN-ONE: 16

Three in PGA Tour events
Four on Senior PGA Tour
One in Japan

ALL-TIME LOW 18-HOLE SCORE: 60

Latrobe Country Club, 1969

SPECIAL GOLF ACHIEVEMENTS

PGA PLAYER OF THE YEAR

1960 and 1962

PGA TOUR LEADING MONEY-WINNER

1958, 1960, 1962, 1963

VARDON TROPHY

1961, 1962, 1964, 1967

RYDER CUP TEAM

1961, 1963, 1965, 1967, 1971, 1973;
Captain – 1963, 1975

CHRYSLER CUP TEAM AND CAPTAIN (SENIOR GOLF)

1966 through 1990

STROKE AVERAGE RECORDS

PGA TOUR INDIVIDUAL EVENTS 1955 THROUGH 1993

Rounds – 2,521
Strokes – 180,110
Average – 71.44

SENIOR PGA TOUR AND OTHER INDIVIDUAL EVENTS OF OFFICIAL NATURE: 1955 THROUGH 1993

Rounds – 688
Strokes – 49,526
Average – 71.98

CAREER HOLES-IN-ONE

1) Latrobe Country Club
   #2, 134 yards, wedge

2) Latrobe Country Club
   #2, 134 yards, wedge

3) Greensburg Country Club
   #16, 9-iron, 1945

4) Desert Inn Country Club, Tournament of Champions, Las Vegas, Nevada
   #16, 6-iron, 1959

5) Pensacola Country Club, Pensacola Open, Pensacola, Florida
   #11, 7-iron, March 3, 1965

6) Johnson City Country Club, Johnson City, Tennessee, Exhibition, 1965

7) Spring Valley Country Club, Sharon, Massachusetts, Exhibition
   #7, 243 yards, 1965

8) Wilmington Country Club, Wilmington, Delaware, Exhibition, 1966

9) Bay Hill Club, Orlando, Florida
   #2 on Charger course, 151 yards, 7-iron, September 27, 1979

10) Indian Wells Country Club, Palm Desert, California, Bob Hope Desert Classic
   #6, 144 yards, 8-iron, January 10, 1980

11) Latrobe Country Club
   #2, 134 yards, Deacon pitching wedge, September 7, 1982

12) Tournament Players Championship at Avenel, Potomac, Maryland, Chrysler Cup Pro-Am
   #3, 182 yards, 5-iron, September 2, 1986

13) Tournament Players Championship at Avenel, Potomac, Maryland, Chrysler Cup Pro-Am
   #3, 182 yards, 5-iron, September 3, 1986

14) Oak Hills Country Club, Narita, Japan, Fuji Electric Grand Slam
   #14, 185 yards, 4-iron, March 25, 1988

15) Tournament Players Championship at Piper Glen, Charlotte, North Carolina, PaineWebber Invitational
   #12, 183 yards, 4-iron, August 5, 1990

16) Inglewood Country Club, Kenmore, Washington, GTE Northwest Classic
   #8, 193 yards, 3-iron, August 21, 1992

Palmer's 12th and 13th holes-in-one
occurred on consecutive days at a pro-am tournament
preceding the 1986 Chrysler Cup.

Photographic references are indicated in bold italics.

FE = Front endsheet   BE = Back endsheet

AUTHOR'S NOTE

In preparing this book, I've gathered material from interviews, books, newspapers, magazines, Arnold Palmer's personal archives in Latrobe and Orlando, and a wide range of other sources. Throughout the manuscript, I've joined separate quotations from the same speaker and excerpted statements to facilitate reporting on a particular thought or event. This editing has been necessary to accommodate the many speakers whose voices are heard and who cover the full scope of Palmer's life. I'm confident that, in so doing, I've done nothing to distort what was said.

Like most authors, I'm indebted to a wide range of people. But I'm particularly indebted to the following individuals who gave generously of their time and knowledge in the form of interviews for the project: *Members of the Palmer family –* Arnold Palmer, Winnie Palmer, Jerry Palmer, Lois Jean Palmer Tilley, Sandy Palmer Sarni, Peg Palmer Wears and Amy Palmer Saunders. *Business associates –* Doc Giffin, Mark McCormack, Alastair Johnston, Barry Frank, Ed Seay, Dick Westman and Darrell Brown. *Fellow golfers –* Jack Nicklaus, Byron Nelson, Sam Snead, Gary Player, Lee Trevino, Dow Finsterwald, Charlie Sifford, Chi Chi Rodriguez and Dave Marr. *Writers and other media representatives –* Herbert Warren Wind, Frank Deford, Jim Murray, Dick Schaap, Bob Costas, Jerry Izenberg, Bob Drum, Ray Cave, Jack Meyers, Dave Kindred, Hugh McIlvanney, Rick Reilly, Bob Sommers, Bert Sugar and Pat Summerall. *Photographers and artists –* Neil Leifer, Walter Iooss, John Zimmerman and Leroy Neiman.

PHOTO CREDITS

AP/WIDE WORLD PHOTOS: inside front cover endsheet, 11, 38, 58, 76, 123, 180 center left; Courtesy of THE ARNOLD PALMER COLLECTION: 1, 5, 9, 13, 20, 22 above, 23 above left, 23 above right, 30, 31, 42, 48, 68 below, 72, 74 above, 83, 127, 132, 133, 145 above, 147, 150, 162, 166, 169, 180 top left, 180 top right, 180 center, 182 above, 183, 186, 187; Courtesy of ARNOLD PALMER ENTERPRISES: 161; BARR, Tom: 182 below left; BATH, Philip/S.I.: 104; BENSON, Harry/Life: inside back cover endsheet; CANNON, David/Allsport: 148 below, 172; CLARKSON, Rich/S.I.: 142 above; CRANHAM, Gerry/S.I.: 143; CULVER PICTURES: 180 top center; Courtesy of the DETROIT FREE PRESS: 24/25; DOMINIS, John/Life: 57, 70/71, 81, 121; DRAKE, James/S.I.: 47, 69, *77, 85, 91, 102, 106/107, 108, 112/113, 114, 137, 139 below, 152, 189; FRANK CHRISTIAN STUDIO: 89; GIGLI, Ormond: 43; GILES, Dr. Howdy: 182 below right, inside back flap; GOMEL, Bob/Life: cover, 32, 40, 41, 54, 64 right, 65, 66/67, 88, 101, 109, 173, back cover; GREHAN, Farrell/S.I.: 16; GUICHARD, Jean/Gamma: 160; HANLON, John D./S.I.: 144; HARE, Clyde/S.I.: 2; HUNTZINGER, Robert/S.I.: 44, 59, 64 left, 68 above, 73, 105; IACONO, John/S.I.: 142 below, 155; IOOSS JR., Walter/S.I.: 17, 75, *77, 93, 99, 111 left, 115, 125, 131, 135; IOOSS JR., Walter: 122, 138, 139 above; IWASAKI, Carl/S.I.: 149; KAMSLER, Leonard: 96, 148 above, 154, 156, 171, 184; KANE, Art/S.I.: 111 right; KLEMME, Mike/Golfoto, Inc.: 153; KLUETMEIER, Heinz/S.I.: 134; LEIFER, Neil/S.I.: 53, 97, 110, 116/117; LEIFER, Neil: 95, 128; LIBERMAN, Frank: 180 bottom left; LOVERO, V.J./S.I.: 174; McCAULEY, Skeet/Image Bank: 163; MEEK, Richard/S.I.: 19, 26/27, 28; NEHAMKIN, Lester: 180 bottom right; NEWMAN, Arnold/S.I.: 126; NEWMAN, Marvin/S.I.: 140/141; Courtesy of THE NORMAN ROCKWELL FAMILY TRUST: 165; O'BRYON, Michael/S.I.: 159; Courtesy of the PGA OF AMERICA: 158; PITTSBURGH POST GAZETTE: 164; POWELL, Mike/Allsport: 185; RICKERBY, Art/S.I.: 55; RUPPEL, Rey/Pat Hathaway Collection of California Views: 15; SCHWEIKARDT, Eric/S.I.: 87, 118; SEED, Brian/S.I.: 60/61, 79, 82; SHAY, Arthur/Life: 34, 35; SILK, George/Life: 50, 51, 52; SMITH, Stuart/S.I.: 120; STRAUSS, Bob: 175, 176; TURNER, Pete/S.I.: 62/63; Courtesy of the UNITED STATES COAST GUARD: 10; Courtesy of the UNITED STATES GOLF ASSOCIATION: 6, 22 below; UPI/ BETTMANN: 29, 130; WALKER, Diana: 170, 181; WHITE HOUSE PHOTO ARCHIVES: 180 center right; WINNERT, Ben: 146; ZIMMERMAN, John/S.I.: 3, 37, 39, 80, 84.

*shared credit   S.I.= Sports Illustrated

OPUS PRODUCTIONS INC.

President/Creative Director:
Derik Murray
Designer:
Dave Mason/Dave Mason & Associates
Picture Editor:
Steve Fine/Sports Illustrated
Assistant Picture Editor:
Miriam Marseu/Sports Illustrated
Design/Production Assistant:
Pamela Lee/Dave Mason & Associates
Artifact Photography:
Derik Murray Photography Inc./Perry Danforth, Grant Waddell, Jason Stroud, with the assistance of T. Alexander Denmarsh, Alex Jones
Vice President, Sales and Marketing:
Glenn McPherson
Marketing Coordinator:
David Attard

Vice President, Director of Publishing:
Marthe Love
Editorial Consultants:
Katherine Zmetana, Jennifer Love
Production Manager:
Paula Guise
Editorial Coordinator:
Wendy Darling
Visual Coordinator:
Colette Aubin
Editorial Research:
David Attard
Production Assistants:
Cathy Love, Deborah Winser
Administrative Assistant:
Robin Evans
Artifact Photography Coordinator:
Andreanne Ricard
Project Accountant:
Kim Steele

Opus Productions would like to thank the following for their dedication and invaluable contribution to the project:

Arnold and Winnie Palmer

Arnold Palmer Enterprises:
Doc Giffin and Jerry Palmer; as well as Arnold Palmer's personal staffs at Latrobe and Bay Hill; and the staff of the Latrobe Country Club.

International Management Group:
Mark McCormack, Alastair J. Johnston, Barry Frank, Trish Lande, Bev Norwood, Georgia Viehbeck, Jane Joseph and Gen Seidell.

CollinsPublishersSanFrancisco:
Jennifer Barry, Maura Carey Damacion, Linda Ferrer, Lynne Noone, Jonathan Mills, Sophie Deprez, Jenny Collins, Jennifer Grace and Julie Bernatz.

Opus Productions would like to acknowledge the following for their assistance and support:
• *KODAK CANADA INC. – all artifacts photographed exclusively on Ektachrome Professional film.*
• *FEDERAL EXPRESS CANADA LTD. – all express delivery shipments worldwide.*
• *Booth Photographic Ltd. – Printfile Archival Preservers*

• Richard J. Ayoub, The Weston Golf and Country Club • Jim Bishop, TGL Sales Ltd. • Dorothy Brown
• George D. Burke, David L. Thomas, Bull, Housser & Tupper • Ray Cave • Dr. Howdy Giles • Bill Gugliotta, *Pittsburgh Post Gazette*
• Jamie Engen, Price Waterhouse • Tracey Kennedy, Arnold Palmer Golf Management Company • Arthur Klebanoff • Hugh McArthur
• Sandy Mitchell, Polaroid Canada • Kathryn Murphy, Augusta National Golf Club • Andrew Mutch, USGA • Bronwen Pencarrick
• Cliff Pickles • Chris Richardson • Peter Scarth, Kodak Canada • Herb Scribe

I always preferred Palmer the sportsman to Palmer the social philosopher. I don't know the man except as an observer. But I have the feeling that he holds a somewhat simplistic view of the world. For most athletes, the heart of talent is luck, and Arnold Palmer was born lucky. Golf is something that he was genetically equipped to do. His good looks were luck. The fact that he had a certain type of upbringing was luck. I'm sure a vast amount of hard work went into everything that Arnold Palmer has accomplished, but no amount of hard work could transform the average person into an Arnold Palmer. And I get the sense that Arnold tends to look at things and say to himself, "Well, I got off my ass and I did it; why can't everyone else?" And that to me is a limited view of the relationship between his own prowess and the rest of the world. One-on-one, I can't imagine Palmer being ugly or mean to anyone because I think he genuinely likes people. But he comes from a world of far greater privilege than he might realize, and he's been so successful as an American hero that he hasn't had to step outside of it. HUGH McILVANNEY I had a last-minute assignment on April 4, 1970. Palmer at that point was an underdog in most tournaments. But after three rounds, he was leading the Greensboro Open; and in mid-afternoon Sports Illustrated learned that he was scheduled to be in Washington that night for a state dinner at the White House with the Duke and Duchess of Windsor. So the magazine asked me to fly down to Dulles Airport and get a photo of Arnold getting out of his jet with Winnie. I went down to Washington, and it was one of those scenes I'll never forget. It was a classic evening; a warm April night. The sun was setting; the sky was full of colors. There was a long limousine waiting on the runway. And in comes this beautiful Learjet that looked like a flying sports car. As the plane got closer, I could see Palmer in the pilot's seat. His collar was open, but he was wearing a tuxedo shirt. The plane came to a halt, and then I saw Winnie inside, wearing a gorgeous evening gown. She handed Arnold his jacket and helped him with his tie. Then he helped her off the plane, posed for several photos for me, and they got in the limousine to go have dinner with the President of the United States. And I said to myself, "This is a real-life James Bond." NEIL LEIFER In 1960, Sports Illustrated chose Arnold as its 'Sportsman of the Year,' and I went to West Virginia, where he was playing in the West Virginia Open, to interview him for the story. It was a good place to talk, because there wasn't much pressure in the tournament and not much competition for Arnold's attention. And I'll never forget; we were in a diner. Arnold was eating a hamburger. There was a bottle of ketchup on the table, and Arnold said to the waitress, "You shouldn't use this kind of ketchup; Heinz is better." After she left, I asked him, "What's with the ketchup?" And he told me, "I have a ketchup contract." But that's the way Arnold was. He really thought that, because he had that contract, he had an obligation to be out there selling Heinz ketchup 24 hours a day. RAY CAVE When I played, like everyone else on the tour, I held down a second job. In the late 1930s when I won the Masters and U.S. Open, I was head pro at a club in Reading, Pennsylvania. And that wasn't just for show; I taught and helped run the pro shop. In 1945, the year I won all those tournaments, I had a job in Toledo, Ohio. And you talk about how things change. In 1945, I did one little commercial, for Wheaties. And even that didn't amount to much, except they gave me a lot of Wheaties to eat. BYRON NELSON In golf, there's a rule that, if you're on the green and there's water between your ball and the hole, you can pace into the hole and then pace out the same number of steps along a dry line so you don't have to putt through the water. And one time, I remember, Arnold and I were partners at the Bing Crosby Pro-Am. There was a lot of water on the greens. And every time Arnold moved his ball, he'd pace into the hole, and then take paces going out that were thirty percent longer than the ones going in, with the result that 10-foot putts became 13-foot putts and so on. And we were together as a team, so it irritated me. I said, "What are you doing?" And he told me, "Mark, if one person around this green thought I was doing it the other way and taking bigger paces going in, I couldn't live with it. I just don't want any misunderstandings." MARK McCORMACK I have a hard time understanding how a batter can stand at home plate with a pitcher throwing a baseball at 90 miles an hour and 50,000 people screaming, "Stick it in his ear," and how Michael Jordan can shoot free throws with everyone behind the basket waving their arms and screaming, "Miss it," but a golfer can't hit a golf ball if someone sneezes. But that's the way it is, so when you're photographing golf, you have to be careful. God forbid, you should move or your camera should go off at the wrong time by accident. Before you know it, some security guard will be hustling you away. Anyway, it's now June 1963, and I've been assigned to cover the Thunderbird Classic. Palmer was hot, so I was following him. It was in the third round, late in the day. He was on a huge green, with his ball on the fringe. I got on the opposite fringe, knelt down on one knee, and lined up my shot with Palmer putting straight toward me. You know how they pace back and forth, look at the putt. He did that; no problem. Then he stood over the putt, looked up, and something was bothering him. He sort of brushed away a fly or something with a gesture of his hand. It looked to me as though he wasn't happy with the line he was taking. I shot a few pictures while I was waiting, and the scene repeated itself several times. Arnold looking at the putt, crouching down, motioning with his hand. Finally, he walked away from the ball entirely, circled around the outside of the green – and this is on live television; it's Arnold Palmer, so you know the cameras are on him. He walks right over to me, crouches down, puts his arm around me, and says, "Listen Neil; do you think you could move four or five feet to the side because you're right in my sight line." I jumped 10 feet. Words can't express how embarrassed I was. But the point is, any other golfer in the world would have shouted "Move!" or "Get that kid out of here!" But even at what was obviously a crucial point in a very important tournament, Palmer was thinking about someone else's feelings. And he won the tournament. NEIL LEIFER Daddy was so involved with golf and traveled so much that he wasn't home a lot when I was growing up. But when he was, he was a strict disciplinarian and I was a bit frightened of him. There were lots of rules; everything from eating what was on our plate to the length our fingernails were supposed to be. In fact, I can remember sometimes making a fist because I didn't want him to see that my fingernails were longer than he allowed them to be. And he was adamant about things like our not wearing makeup, how we should dress, the way we cut our hair. Details were important, and to this day he's still very opinionated about how we live our lives and the things we do and say. But it was wonderful growing up in Latrobe. It's a small town, and because Daddy had lived there all his life, people there were proud of him but not awestruck. He was just one of the guys in Latrobe, and that made our own childhood as normal as it could be. We weren't treated like the children of a big celebrity. Our lives were private. And as I've grown older, especially now that I have four children of my own, I've come to understand how hard he and my mom worked for Peg and me. I suppose in some ways Daddy has mellowed in recent years. And I think he's been able to enjoy my children more than he enjoyed Peg and me, because he has more time now to spend with family. But he's still basically the same person he always was; he just shows it differently. And he's a very special person. I couldn't ask for finer parents or a better life than the one they've given me. AMY PALMER SAUNDERS